Real-Life English

A COMPETENCY–BASED ESL PROGRAM FOR ADULTS

Program Consultants

Jayme Adelson-Goldstein
North Hollywood Learning Center
North Hollywood, California

Julia Collins
Los Angeles Unified School District
El Monte-Rosemead Adult School
El Monte, California

Else V. Hamayan
Illinois Resource Center
Des Plaines, Illinois

Kent Heitman
Carver Community Middle School
Delray Beach, Florida

Patricia De Hesus-Lopez
Texas A & M University
Kingsville, Texas

Federico Salas-Isnardi
Houston Community College
Adult Literacy Programs
Houston, Texas

Connie Villaruel
El Monte-Rosemead Adult School
El Monte, California

Wei-hua (Wendy) Wen
Adult & Continuing Education
New York City Board of Education
New York, New York

STECK-VAUGHN
COMPANY
A Subsidiary of National Education Corporation

ACKNOWLEDGMENTS

Staff Credits:

Executive Editor ◆ Ellen Lehrburger
Senior Editor ◆ Tim Collins
Design Manager ◆ Richard Balsam
Cover Design ◆ Richard Balsam

Photo Credits:
Cover: © Randal Alhadeff, Cooke Photographics (title).

Illustration Credits:
The Ivy League of Artists, Inc.

Additional Illustration by:
Scott Bieser–p.62a-c, 62e-j, 63b, 63c, 63e, 63f, 63h, 63i, 63k, 63l, 63n, 63o, 64c-e, 65b-g, 67b, 69a, 69b, 69f-h, 69j, 70c, 70f, 70g, 70i, 70l, 71b, 71c, 71g-i, 72b, 72d, 72h, 74b, 75b, 75e, 77b, 83d; D. Childress–p.98d, 107e, 107f; Rhonda Childress–p.8c, 8d, 30a, 38b-d, 40c, 64a, 64b; Adolph Gonzalez–p.66c, 67a, 67c, 90c, 91c, 91f, 95b, 95f, 106, 144g, 149h, 150; David Griffin–p.76f-j, 76l, 76m, 81b, 81d, 81f, 81h, 83f, 83g, 122a-h, 122j-l, 123, 128a, 130, 131a-d, 146; Lyda Guz–p.48d; John Harrison–p.74c-e, 75a, 75c, 75d, 76b-e, 76k-m, 81f, 83b, 83c, 83e-g, 90b, 90d-g, 91a, 91b, 91d, 91e, 91g, 91h, 91j-m, 95a, 95c-e, 96a, 96b, 96e, 96g, 96h, 98a, 99a-c, 107a-c, 122c, 122i, 144c, 144d, 144f, 145, 149a-g, 149i ; Michael Krone–p.12, 14, 16, 18, 50a, 52, 54, 56; Yvette Scott–p.112; Keith Wilson–p.8a, 8b, 23, 32d, 32e, 38a, 40a, 40b, 40d, 42, 44a, 44b, 45a-e, 47a, 47b, 48c, 66a, 72a, 74a, 75f, 78, 80, 83a, 88, 90a, 96c, 96d, 99d, 100-104, 107d, 108, 110, 111, 114, 120, 127a.

About The Writers:

Student Book ◆ Sarah Cogliano
Sarah Cogliano holds a B.A. degree from Wellesley College, Wellesley, Massachusetts. She has taught ESL/EFL to adults in Guadalajara, Mexico, Boston, Massachusetts, and Austin, Texas. Ms. Cogliano currently specializes in materials development for ESL and Adult Basic Education.

Teacher's Edition ◆ Judy Veramendi
Judy Veramendi holds a degree from the Universidad de Navarra, Pamplona, Spain. She has taught ESL at all levels to children and adults. Ms. Veramendi currently specializes in materials development.

Electronic Production:
International Electronic Publishing Center, Inc.

ISBN 0-8114-3216-5

CONTENTS

LITERACY LEVEL

Units	Competencies	Recognition Words
Introductory Unit	Use left-to-right and top-to-bottom progression Identify, say, and write letters **a** through **z** Identify, say, and write numerals **0** through **90** Discriminate among lower-case letters Discriminate among capital letters Match capital and lower-case letters Read direction lines used throughout the book	listen ◆ look ◆ say ◆ raise your hand ◆ circle ◆ write ◆ underline ◆ work with a partner
Personal Communication	Ask for and give personal information Complete a simple form Introduce oneself	address ◆ city ◆ first name ◆ last name ◆ name ◆ number ◆ state ◆ street ◆ telephone number ◆ zip code
Our Community	Identify places Say where places are Buy stamps and mail letters Understand emergency words Report emergencies by telephone	accident ◆ ambulance ◆ bank ◆ fire ◆ fire department ◆ hospital ◆ mailbox ◆ police station ◆ post office ◆ school ◆ stamp
School and Country	Identify people and places at school Say room numbers Identify classroom objects	board ◆ book ◆ country ◆ desk ◆ library ◆ men's room ◆ office ◆ room ◆ student ◆ teacher ◆ women's room
Daily Living	Ask for, say, and write the time Ask for, say, and write the day of the week Ask for, say, and write the date	date ◆ date of birth ◆ days of the week ◆ month ◆ time ◆ today ◆ tomorrow ◆ year
Food	Identify kinds of food Identify kinds of food packaging Ask where things are in a store Comparison shop	aisle ◆ bag ◆ bottle ◆ box ◆ dairy ◆ food ◆ fruit and vegetables ◆ juice ◆ meat ◆ sale ◆ supermarket ◆ $ ◆ ¢
Shopping	Identify kinds of clothes Ask how much something costs Understand amounts of money Read size tags, price tags, and receipts Write checks Ask to return something	cash ◆ cents ◆ charge ◆ check ◆ dollar ◆ driver's license ◆ ID ◆ receipt ◆ $ ◆ ¢
Home	Say where they live Identify kinds of housing Identify furniture and rooms Read for-rent signs Ask about the rent and the deposit	apartment ◆ bathroom ◆ bed ◆ bedroom ◆ chair ◆ deposit ◆ house ◆ kitchen ◆ lamp ◆ living room ◆ refrigerator ◆ rent ◆ sofa ◆ stove ◆ table
Health Care	Identify parts of the body Describe symptoms and injuries Read medicine labels Make doctors' appointments	arm ◆ capsule ◆ cold ◆ cough ◆ fever ◆ flu ◆ foot ◆ hand ◆ headache ◆ leg ◆ medicine ◆ sick ◆ sore throat ◆ stomach-ache ◆ tablespoon ◆ tablet ◆ teaspoon
Employment	Identify kinds of jobs Give their work experience Give and follow instructions Read help-wanted signs Complete a simple job application	application ◆ days ◆ experience ◆ help wanted ◆ job ◆ nights ◆ pay ◆ weekends
Transportation	Identify kinds of transportation Read traffic signs Ask for schedule and fare information	bicycle ◆ bus ◆ bus stop ◆ car ◆ don't walk ◆ drive ◆ fare ◆ no parking ◆ one way ◆ ride ◆ speed limit ◆ stop ◆ subway ◆ train ◆ walk

Units	Competencies	Grammar
LEVEL 1		
Personal Communication	Ask for and give personal information Say hello Introduce oneself Complete an identification form	Present tense of **be,** statements Subject pronouns Possessive adjectives Questions with **where + from**
Our Community	Identify places Tell where places are Read maps Ask for, give, and follow directions Use a pay phone to report an emergency	Present tense of **be** **yes/no** questions, short answers Prepositions of location **A/an** Questions with **where**

School and Country	Listen for room numbers
	Identify people and places at school
	Talk about where places are in buildings
	Read building directories
	Write absentee notes
		Present progressive tense
		  statements, negatives, **yes/no**
		  questions, short answers
		Questions with **what** and **where**
		Possessive nouns

Daily Living	Talk about seasons and weather
	Ask for, say, and write times and dates
	Read calendars
	Listen for times and dates
	Listen to weather forecasts
	Read store hour signs
		Expressions with **it**
		  statements, negatives, questions,
		  short answers

Food	Identify kinds of food Write shopping lists Identify food packaging Ask where things are in a supermarket Listen for aisle numbers Read price tags and expiration dates	Singular and plural nouns Mass/count distinction **A/an** or **some** Questions with **how much** and **how many**

Shopping	Identify clothes by article, size, and color
	Shop for clothes
	Write checks
	Read clothing ads and comparison shop
	Listen for and say prices and totals
	Read size tags, price tags, and receipts
		This/that/these/those
		Simple present tense
		  statements, negatives, questions,
		  short answers

Home	Identify rooms, furniture, and housing
	Read for-rent ads
	Ask for utilities to be turned on
	Ask for simple repairs
		There's/there are
		  statements, negatives, questions,
		  short answers
		Prepositions of location

Health Care	Identify kinds of health clinics Read a thermometer Make doctors' appointments Talk about symptoms and injuries Listen to doctors' instructions	Simple present tense of **have** Simple present tense of **feel** Questions with **how**

Employment	Identify kinds of jobs
	Give their work experience and skills
	Read help-wanted ads
	Complete job applications
	Understand safety warnings
		Can, statements, negatives, questions,
		  short answers
		Simple past tense of **be**
		Questions with **how long;** answers with
		  for/from…to

Transportation and Travel	Identify kinds of transportation Read traffic signs Use public transportation Listen for bus numbers and fares	Simple present and present progressive tenses (review and contrast) Questions with **which**

LEVEL 2

Units	Competencies	Grammar
Personal Communication	Identify people in their families Give personal information Introduce people Describe people Apply for a driver's license	Present tense of **be** (review) Simple present tense (review) Present tense of **have** (review) Object pronouns
Our Community	Identify bank services Complete deposit and withdrawal slips Listen for amounts due Buy money orders Buy stamps and send packages	Simple past tense statements, negatives, **wh-** questions Irregular verbs in the simple past tense
Our Country	Identify branches of government Identify citizenship requirements Complete a citizenship application Describe the U.S. flag Say the Pledge of Allegiance	Contrast of simple present and present progressive tenses (review) **Have to** **(I)'d like to**

Daily Living	Describe their native countries
	Talk about why they came to the U.S.
	Describe how they felt when they came
	   to the U.S.
	Talk about where they have lived
		Simple past tense
		   wh- questions, **yes/no** questions,
		   short answers
		More irregular verbs in the simple past
		   tense

Food	Read recipes and package directions Listen to supermarket ads Read supermarket ads Identify sales and coupons	**Some** and **any** statements, negatives, questions Imperatives
Shopping	Comparison shop Identify forms of payment Ask for refunds and exchanges Identify sales tax Read clothing care labels	Comparative adjectives with **-er** and **more**
Home	Talk about housing and neighborhoods Read for-rent ads Complete a change of address form Read utility bills	Adverbials of location Questions and short answers with **there**
Health Care	Identify kinds of doctors Talk about symptoms and medicine Identify practices that lead to good health Complete medical history forms Listen to doctors' advice Read medicine labels	**Should/shouldn't** Conditional sentences with **should** or with imperatives
Employment	Ask about job openings Interview for a job ♦ Accept a job offer Complete a Social Security form Listen to instructions at work Explain absences from work	Polite requests with **could** Clauses with **so** and **because**
Transportation and Travel	Talk about getting a driver's license Identify safe driving practices Identify car maintenance procedures Ask for and give road directions Read road maps	**Should/shouldn't** (review) **Have to** (review) Conditional sentences with **should** or with imperatives (review) Clauses with **so** and **because** (review)

LEVEL 3

Units	Competencies	Grammar
Personal Communication	Identify recreational activities Listen to taped announcements Interpret recreational schedules Complete registration forms	**And/or/but** Gerunds and infinitives
Our Community	Report utility problems Use the telephone directory Identify community service agencies Leave and take telephone messages Check telephone bills	Object pronouns with **for** and **to** **Should/shouldn't** (review)
Our Country	Read weather maps Understand U.S. geography Read weather reports Listen to weather reports	Expressions with **it** (review) Future with **going to** Adverbs with **-ly**
Daily Living	Identify community issues Identify community groups Write to elected officials Interpret cost-of-living charts	Present perfect tense with **for** and **since** 　statements, negatives, **yes/no** 　questions, short answers Irregular past participles Reporting speech in the present tense
Food	Read menus Order in restaurants Talk about food preferences Identify the basic food groups	Linking verbs Comparative adjectives with **-er** and **more** 　(review) Superlative adjectives with **-est** and **most**
Shopping	Identify kinds of stores Read a catalog Order by mail Identify clothes by article, size, and material	Nouns used as adjectives Sequence of modification
Home	Talk about household maintenance Understand home safety precautions Ask for household repairs Read public service ads Read product labels	Clauses with **when/while** and the 　simple past/past progressive tenses Clauses with **before/after** and the 　simple past tense **Make/do**
Health Care	Report accidents Call the poison control center Listen to first-aid instructions Read first-aid product packages Understand first-aid procedures	Reflexive pronouns Conditional sentences with **will**
Employment	Report whether work is complete Identify work safety equipment Listen to safety instructions at work Read notices at work Check paychecks	Simple past tense with **ago** Present perfect tense with **already** 　and **yet**
Transportation and Travel	Make travel plans and buy tickets Identify kinds of transportation Listen to travel announcements Check travel tickets	Future with **going to** (review) Conditional sentences with **will** (review) Present perfect tense with **ever/never**

LEVEL 4

Units	Competencies	Grammar

Personal Communication	Offer invitations
	Accept invitations
	Turn down invitations
	Write invitations
		Present tenses (review)
		   present tense of **be**, simple present,
		   present progressive
		Feel (review)

Our Community	Endorse checks
	Pay by check
	Compare bank services
	Balance checkbooks
		Past tenses (review)
		   simple past, past progressive
		Clauses with **when** and **while**
		Used to
		   statements, questions

Our Country	Read about U.S. history Understand the U.S. Constitution Understand equal educational opportunity	Simple past tense with **ago** (review) Present perfect tense with **for** and **since**
Daily Living	Identify environmental problems Identify community problems Read about environmental solutions	Passive voice (simple present, simple past) Gerunds and infinitives as objects
Food	Identify kinds of stores Understand unit cost Read ingredients on food packages	Gerunds as objects of prepositions **It's** + adjective + infinitive
Shopping	Identify kinds of stores Read garage sale ads Write garage sale ads Read warranties	**Wh-** questions (review) Restrictive relative clauses
Home	Correct household hazards Request repairs Write complaint letters Read leases	**Must/may** Gerunds as subjects Conditional sentences with **could**
Health Care	Identify good health habits Answer a doctor's questions Compare and choose insurance plans Complete insurance claim forms	**Must be** (possibility) **Should/ought to/had better** (advice)
Employment	Talk about education, work experience, and career plans Identify traits of good employees Talk about rules at work Identify job benefits	Gerunds as subjects and objects (review) Present and past participles
Transportation and Travel	Understand car maintenance and repair Identify safe driving practices Complete customer complaint forms Read auto product labels	Present perfect tense (review)

Real-Life English is a complete competency-based, four-skill program for teaching ESL to adults and young adults. The program is designed for students enrolled in public or private schools, in learning centers, or in institutes, or for individuals working with tutors. *Real-Life English* consists of four levels plus a Literacy Level for use prior to or together with Level 1.

◆ FEATURES

♦ ***Real-Life English* is competency-based.** *Real-Life English's* competency-based syllabus gives adult students the life skills they need to succeed in the U.S. The syllabus is compatible with the CASAS Competencies, the Mainstream English Language Training Project (MELT), and with state curriculums for adult ESL from Texas and California.

The *About You* symbol appears on the Student Book page each time students use a competency. These activities are always personalized and communicative or life-skill based.

♦ ***Real-Life English* is communicative.** Numerous conversational models and communicative activities—including mixers, problem-solving activities, and information-gap activities—get students talking from the start.

♦ ***Real-Life English* addresses all four language skills.** Listening, speaking, reading, and writing are developed in separate sections in each unit. In addition, competency-based Word Bank and Structure Base sections in each unit develop the vocabulary and grammar students need.

♦ ***Real-Life English* is appropriate for adults.** The language and situations presented in *Real-Life English* are ones adults are likely to encounter in the U.S. The abundance of attractive, true-to-life photographs, illustrations, and realia will interest and motivate adults.

♦ ***Real-Life English* starts at the appropriate level for beginning students.** The Literacy Level is designed for students who have no prior knowledge of English and have few or no literacy skills in their native language(s) or are literate in a language with a non-Roman alphabet. Level 1 is intended for students with little or no prior knowledge of English. As students continue through the program, they reach progressively higher levels of language and life-skills. For information on placement, see page vi of the Introduction To The Literacy Level.

♦ ***Real-Life English* is appropriate for multi-level classes.** Because unit topics carry over from level to level, the series is ideal for use in multi-level classes. Units are situational and non-sequential, making *Real-Life English* appropriate for open-entry/open-exit situations.

COMPONENTS

Real-Life English consists of:

- ♦ Five Student Books (Literacy and Levels 1–4)

- ♦ Four Workbooks (Levels 1–4)

- ♦ Five Teacher's Editions (Literacy and Levels 1–4)

- ♦ Audiocassettes (Literacy and Levels 1–4)

Student Books

Each two-color Student Book consists of ten fourteen-page units. (Units are twelve pages each in the Literacy Level.) Each unit is organized around a single competency-based topic, providing students with ample time on task to acquire the target competencies and language.

♦ **For easy teaching and learning, the Student Books follow a consistent format.** Each book has ten consistently organized units, each of which can be taught in approximately six to ten classroom sessions. In addition, each unit follows a consistent pattern. For more information, see page iv of the Introduction To The Literacy Level.

♦ **A separate Literacy Level Student Book builds literacy and life skills.** Students learn foundation literacy skills in tandem with listening and speaking skills. The competency-based syllabus ensures that students get the life skills they need to live in the U.S.

♦ **Clear directions, abundant examples, and pedagogical use of color assure that students always know exactly what**

to do. Boldface type is used in direction lines to make them easy for students to find and read. Exercises examples make tasks clear to students and teachers. To facilitate personalization, color is used in dialogs and exercises to indicate words that students are to change when they are talking or writing about themselves.

♦ **Check Your Competency pages provide a complete evaluation program.** Teachers can use these pages to evaluate students' progress and to track the program's learner verification needs. Success is built in because competencies are always checked in familiar formats.

Workbooks

The Workbooks for Levels 1–4 contain ten eight-page units plus a complete Answer Key at the back of each book. Each Workbook unit contains at least one exercise for each section of the Student Book. To allow for additional reinforcement of vocabulary and structure, there are multiple exercises for Word Bank and Structure Base.

Teacher's Editions

The complete Teacher's Editions help both new and experienced teachers organize their teaching, motivate their students, and successfully use a variety of individual, pair, and group activities.

♦ **Unit Overviews provide valuable information on how to motivate students and organize teaching.** Each Unit Overview contains an optional Unit Warm-Up teachers can use to build students' interest and get them ready for the unit. Each opener also contains a list of optional materials— including pictures, flash cards, and realia—teachers can use to enliven instruction throughout the entire unit.

♦ **The Teacher's Editions contain complete suggested procedures for every part of the Student Book.** Each section of a unit begins with a list of the competencies developed on the Student Book page(s). Teachers can use this list when planning lessons. Then teaching notes give suggestions for a recommended three-part lesson format:

Preparation: Suggestions for preteaching the new language, competencies, and concepts on the Student Book page(s).

Presentation: Suggested procedures for working with the Student Book page(s) in class.

Follow-Up: A suggested optional activity teachers can use to provide additional reinforcement or to enrich and extend the new language and competencies. The Follow-Ups include a variety of interactive pair and small group activities, as well as numerous reading and writing activities. Each activity has a suggested variant, marked with ♦, for use with students who require activities at a slightly more sophisticated level. For teaching ease, the corresponding Workbook exercise(s) for each page or section of the Student Book are indicated on the Teacher's Edition page.

♦ **The Teacher's Editions contain numerous Teaching Notes, Culture Notes, and Language Notes.** Teachers can share this wealth of information with students or use it in lesson planning.

♦ **Each Teacher's Edition unit concludes with English in Action, an optional holistic cooperative learning project.** Students will find these to be valuable and stimulating culminating activities.

♦ **Additional features.** A Listening Transcript is in each Teacher's Edition. The Teacher's Editions also contain Individual Competency Charts for each unit and a Class Cumulative Competency Chart for teachers to record students' progress and to track the program's learner verification needs.

Audiocassettes

▭ The Audiocassettes at each level contain all dialogs and listening activities marked with this cassette symbol in the Student Book. The Audiocassettes give students experience in listening to a variety of native speakers in authentic situations. The Listening Transcript in each Student Book and Teacher's Edition contains scripts for all listening selections not appearing directly on the pages of the Student Books.

Real-Life English

A COMPETENCY–BASED ESL PROGRAM FOR ADULTS

Program Consultants

Jayme Adelson-Goldstein
North Hollywood Learning Center
North Hollywood, California

Patricia De Hesus-Lopez
Texas A & M University
Kingsville, Texas

Julia Collins
Los Angeles Unified School District
El Monte-Rosemead Adult School
El Monte, California

Federico Salas-Isnardi
Houston Community College
Adult Literacy Programs
Houston, Texas

Else V. Hamayan
Illinois Resource Center
Des Plaines, Illinois

Connie Villaruel
El Monte-Rosemead Adult School
El Monte, California

Kent Heitman
Carver Community Middle School
Delray Beach, Florida

Wei-hua (Wendy) Wen
Adult & Continuing Education
New York City Board of Education
New York, New York

STECK-VAUGHN
C O M P A N Y
A Subsidiary of National Education Corporation

Real-Life English is a complete competency-based, four-skill program for teaching ESL to adults and young adults. *Real-Life English* follows a competency-based syllabus that is compatible with the CASAS and MELT competencies, as well as state curriculums for adult ESL from Texas and California. The program is designed for students enrolled in public or private schools, learning centers, or institutes, and for individuals working with tutors.

The program consists of four levels plus this Literacy Level. The Literacy Level is intended for use with students who have no prior knowledge of English and few or no literacy skills in their own language(s). It is also designed for use with students who are literate in a language with a non-Roman alphabet. Because unit topics carry over from other levels of *Real-Life English,* the Literacy Level can be used prior to or with Level 1.

Real-Life English has these components:

♦ Five Student Books (Literacy and Levels 1–4).

♦ Five Teacher's Editions (Literacy and Levels 1–4), which provide detailed suggestions on how to present each section of the Student Book in class.

♦ Four Workbooks (Levels 1–4), which provide reinforcement for each section of Student Books 1–4.

♦ Two Audiocassettes at each level (Literacy and Levels 1–4), which contain all dialogs and listening activities in the Student Books. This symbol indicates all of the activities for which material is recorded on the Audiocassettes. A transcript of all material recorded on the tapes but not appearing directly on the Student Book pages is at the back of each Student Book and Teacher's Edition.

◆ Organization of the Literacy Level Student Book

Real-Life English Literacy Level consists of a ten-page Introductory Unit and ten units of instruction. The competencies for each unit are listed by unit in the Table of Contents. Teachers can use this list for lesson planning and for learner verification.

Introductory Unit

The Introductory Unit presents left-to-right progression, top-to-bottom progression, number formation, letter formation, letter discrimination and capital/lower case letter correspondence. In addition, the Introductory Unit uses captioned pictures to present the direction lines in the rest of the book. A page lined with wide (primary) rules is also provided for teachers and/or students to duplicate and use for additional writing practice. (Teachers can also use copies of this page to create their own worksheets. Write the words, letters, or sentences students need to practice on a copy of the page. Then duplicate it for students.)

The Introductory Unit can be used in several ways. Teachers can present any or all of the pages before students begin Unit 1. Or teachers might have students turn back to these pages for extra reinforcement as the class works through each unit. Because the Introductory Unit can be used at any point in the book, *Real-Life English* Literacy Level is ideal for open-entry/open-exit programs.

Units 1–10

Units 1–10 follow a competency-based syllabus that presents foundation literacy skills in tandem with listening and speaking skills. Thus, students simultaneously develop the language and life skills they need to live in the U.S.

The *About You* symbol, a unique feature, appears on the Student Book page each time students use a competency independently.

Blackline Masters and Listening Transcript

At the end of the book, Blackline Masters for each unit allow for valuable reinforcement and enrichment of instruction. The Listening Transcript presents all of the listening activities not appearing directly on the Student Book pages.

Organization of a Unit

Each of the ten units follows a consistent whole-part-whole organization:

♦ The Unit Opener presents an overview of the unit topic and competencies.

♦ Four to five teaching spreads systematically present the new material in the unit.

♦ The Put It Together, Check Your Competency, and Extension pages allow for integration, evaluation, and expansion of the new language and competencies.

Unit Opener

Each Unit Opener of *Real-Life English* Literacy Level includes a large, engaging illustration and accompanying questions. Each illustration depicts people using the unit's target language, literacy skills, and competencies. Situations include people applying for jobs, completing forms, shopping for food or clothing, finding homes, or seeing doctors. The illustration and questions activate students' prior knowledge by getting them to think and talk about the unit topic. To stimulate discussion, follow these suggestions:

♦ Encourage students to say whatever they can about the illustration. Prompt them by indicating objects for them to name. You might also identify and say the names of objects, places, and people for them to repeat. Write key words on the board.

♦ Help students read any signs or words that are visible.

♦ Have students answer the questions. Repeat their answers or restate them in acceptable English.

Teaching Spreads

Each of the four to five teaching spreads presents one or more literacy and life skills. *Real-Life English* Literacy Level takes a recognition-word approach to teach letters, words, and competencies in meaningful, communicative contexts. Students learn to read and write only the words that they need to know to accomplish the unit competencies.

♦ The recognition words for each spread are presented at the top of the first page of each spread. For information on presenting recognition words, see "Presenting Recognition Words" on page vii.

♦ The first activity on each spread is a short dialog that presents recognition words in context. As students listen to and say each dialog, they gain valuable experience using the new language. For detailed instructions, see "Presenting Dialogs" on page vii.

♦ Exercises give students experience in reading and writing the recognition words in isolation and in context.

♦ The complete alphabet is presented in the first five units in groups of one or two letters on each spread. The letters are always the initial letters of the spread's recognition words. Thus, learning the alphabet becomes a meaningful, relevant task. Exercises give students experience in writing the letters in isolation and in familiar contexts. For suggestions on teaching the letters, see "Presenting Letters" on page vii.

♦ Listening and speaking activities appear on all the spreads, allowing students to develop all four language skills. The paired speaking activities get students talking from the start. Listening tasks include listening for addresses, telephone numbers, prices, directions, and doctors' instructions.

All of the listening activities develop the skill of **focused listening.** Students learn to recognize the information they need and listen selectively for only that information. They do not have to understand every word; rather, they have to filter out everything except the information that they want to find out. This essential skill is used by native speakers of all languages when listening in their own language.

♦ Culminating activities on each spread allow students to use their new literacy skills to read or fill in a piece of realia, such as a job application, a supermarket ad, a check, a receipt, a help-wanted ad, or a bus sign.

Put It Together

The communicative, integrative activities on the Put It Together page allow students to use the new language and competencies for the unit in a holistic reading/writing activity, such as reading a sale ad, completing a job application, reading medicine package labels, and writing checks.

Check Your Competency

The Check Your Competency page is designed to allow teachers to track students' progress and to meet their school's or program's learner verification needs. Skills are tested in the same manner that they were presented in the units, so formats are familiar and non-threatening, and success is built in. For more information on this section, see "Evaluation" on page vii.

Extension

The Extension page enriches the previous instruction with language puzzles, games, and other activities. As students complete these enjoyable activities, they gain additional experience in using the unit's target language and competencies.

Placement

Any number of measures can be used to place students in the appropriate level of *Real-Life English.* This table indicates placement based on the CASAS and MELT-SPL standards.

Student Performance Levels	CASAS Achievement Score	*Real-Life English*
	164 or under	Literacy
I	165–185	Level 1
II	186–190	
III	191–196	Level 2
IV	197–205	
V	206–210	Level 3
VI	211–216	
VII	217–225	Level 4
VIII	226 (+)	

Using this Book in Multi-Level Classes

Real-Life English Literacy Level can be used in a variety of ways in multi-level classes. Here is a suggested procedure.

♦ Present to the class as a whole the oral and aural activities for the day in Level 1 of *Real-Life English.*

♦ Meet with the literacy students as a group for their reading and writing practice as the Level 1 students complete the exercises in their Student Books and Workbooks.

♦ When the literacy students are ready to begin the independent or paired activities in their books, check the Level 1 students' work or provide them with additional instruction.

Teaching Techniques

Presenting Dialogs

To present the dialogs, follow these suggested steps.

♦ Establish meaning by having students talk about the illustration. Clarify all the new vocabulary in the dialog using pictures and pantomime.

♦ Play the tape or say the dialog aloud two or more times.

♦ Say the dialog aloud line-by-line for students to repeat chorally and then individually.

♦ Have students say the dialog together in pairs.

♦ Have several pairs say the dialog aloud for the class.

Presenting Recognition Words

To present each recognition word, first clarify the meaning of the word. Display the object or a picture card, or use the picture on the Student Book page. Say the word and have students repeat. Then display a word card with the word on it. Say the word. As you say it, sweep your hand under the word. Have students repeat. Call attention to the initial letter. Display the word card and the picture card at random and have the class say or read the word chorally each time. Continue until the class can respond with ease. Then have individuals respond.

Reinforcing Vocabulary

To provide additional reinforcement of the recognition words, use any of these suggestions.

♦ **Personal picture dictionaries.** Students can start personal dictionaries in their notebooks. For each new word they can draw or glue in a picture of the object or action.

♦ **Flash cards.** Flash cards are easy for teachers or for students to make. Write a new word or phrase on the front of each card. Put a picture of the object or action on the back of the card. Students can use the cards to review vocabulary or to play a variety of games, such as Concentration.

♦ **The Remember-It Game.** Use this simple memory game to review vocabulary of any topic. For example, to reinforce food words, start the game by saying, *We're having a picnic, and we're bringing apples.* The next student has to repeat what you said and add an item. If someone cannot remember the whole list or cannot add a word, he or she has to drop out. The student who can remember the longest list wins.

Presenting Letters

Use letter cards with both capital and lower-case letters on them to present the letters. Hold up each card, say the name of the letter, and have students repeat. Point out the difference between capital and lower-case letters. Write the capital and lower-case letters on the board and trace them with your finger. Have students trace the strokes in the air. Next have students open their books and trace the letters with their fingers and then with their pencils. Then have them write the letters on the lines.

Presenting Listening Activities

Use any of these suggestions to present the listening activities.

♦ Help students read the directions and the example.

♦ Model the activity. Write the example item on the board and complete it as you play the tape or read the Listening Transcript of the first item aloud. In activities in which students listen and raise their hands, model raising your hand as students observe.

♦ Play the tape or read the Listening Transcript aloud as students complete the activity. Rewind the tape and play it again as necessary.

♦ Check students' work.

Evaluation

To use the Check Your Competency page successfully, follow these suggested procedures. Before and during each evaluation, create a relaxed, affirming atmosphere. Chat with the students for a few minutes and review the material with them. When you and the students are ready, help students read the directions and look over each exercise before they complete it. Make sure that everyone has a pen or a pencil. Then have students complete the activity. If at any time during the process you sense that students are becoming frustrated, feel free to stop the evaluation process to provide additional review. You might have students turn back to the page where the material was presented. Resume when students are ready. Check students' work. The Teacher's Edition contains reproducible charts for you to copy and use to keep track of individual and class progress.

Introductory Unit

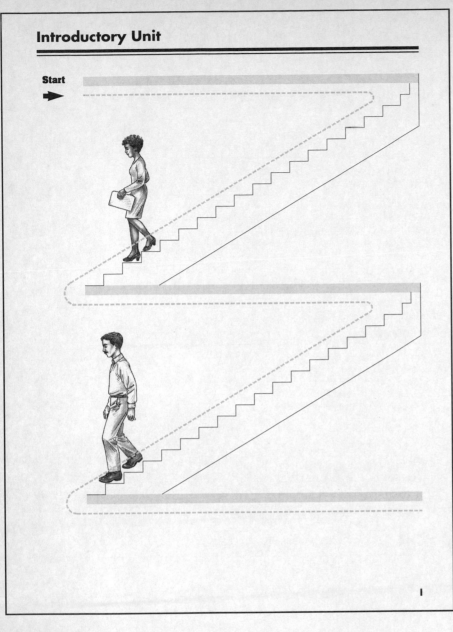

Start

I

PROCEDURES

Draw the dotted line and staircase on the board or overhead projector and demonstrate tracing the line with your finger or a pencil. Then have students start at the arrow and trace the dotted line on the page with their fingers and/or with their pencils. Then have them trace the line in the air with their fingers and/or with their pencils. Finally, have students follow the line with their eyes only.

OBJECTIVE

Use left-to-right and top-to-bottom progression.

OBJECTIVE

Identify, say, and write letters
   a through **m.**

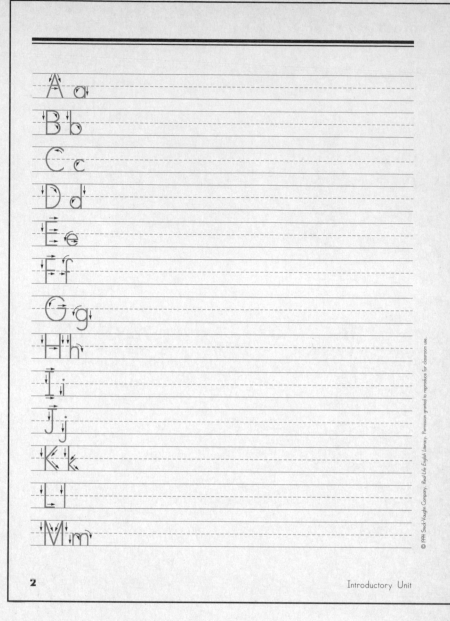

PROCEDURES

Teaching Note: This page can be presented before beginning Unit 1, and/or it can be used for reinforcement as the letters are taught within the units.

Introduce the letters, three at a time. Use flash cards to identify each letter. Hold up the flash card and say the letter. Have students repeat. Point out the differences between the capital and the lower-case letters.

Have students open their books and trace the target letters with their fingers. Suggest that they follow the direction of the arrows. Then have them trace the letters with their pencils. You may also ask them to trace the letters in the air with their fingers or pencils.

Demonstrate copying the letters on the board or overhead projector. Then have students copy the letters. Check each student's work and provide immediate feedback. For additional reinforcement, use page 10 of this unit.

OBJECTIVE
Identify, say, and write letters
n through **z.**

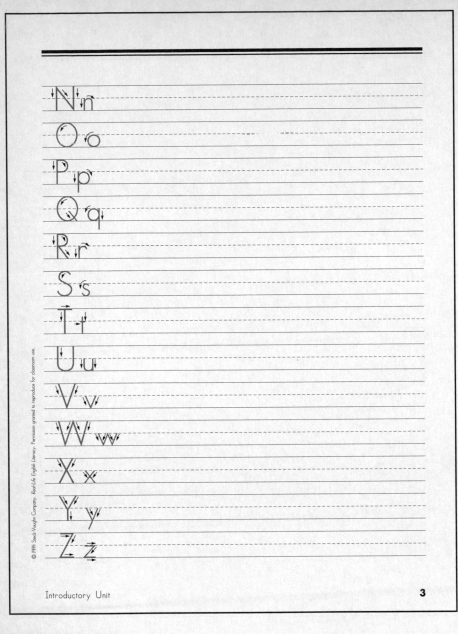

Introductory Unit   **3**

PROCEDURES

Follow the instructions on page 2.

OBJECTIVE

Identify, say, and write numerals
0 through **30**.

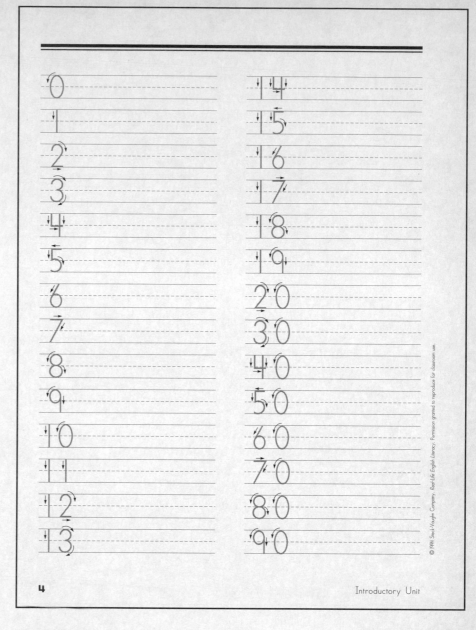

PROCEDURES

Introduce the numerals, three at a time. Use flash cards to identify each number. Hold up the flash card and say the number. Have students repeat.

Have students open their books and trace the target numbers with their fingers. Suggest that they follow the direction of the arrows. Then have them trace the numbers with their pencils. You may also ask them to trace the numbers in the air with their fingers or pencils.

Demonstrate copying the numbers on the board or overhead projector. Then have students copy the numbers. Check each student's work and provide immediate feedback. For additional reinforcement, use page

10 of this unit.

Teaching Note: This page can be presented before beginning Unit 1, and/or it can be used for reinforcement as the numbers are presented within the units.

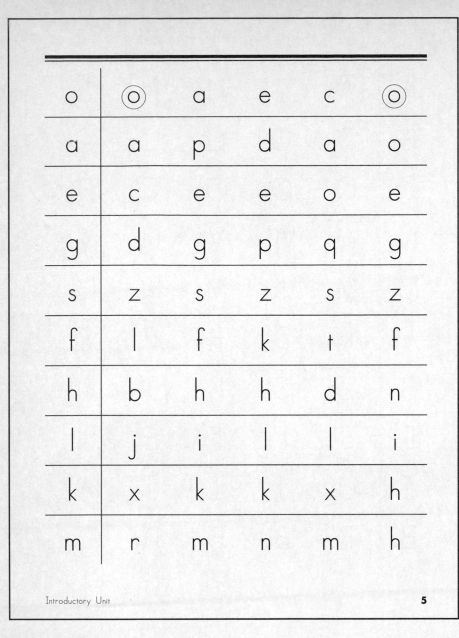

PROCEDURES

Ask volunteers to read the lines of
letters aloud. Demonstrate the first
item on the board or overhead projector. Indicate the letter **o**, then find
and circle the two matching letters in
the line to the right. Have the students complete the exercise independently. Correct the exercise on the
board or overhead projector. Check
each student's work and provide
immediate feedback.

Teaching Note: You may want to
prepare similar pages with other letters for additional reinforcement.

OBJECTIVES

Discriminate among capital letters.

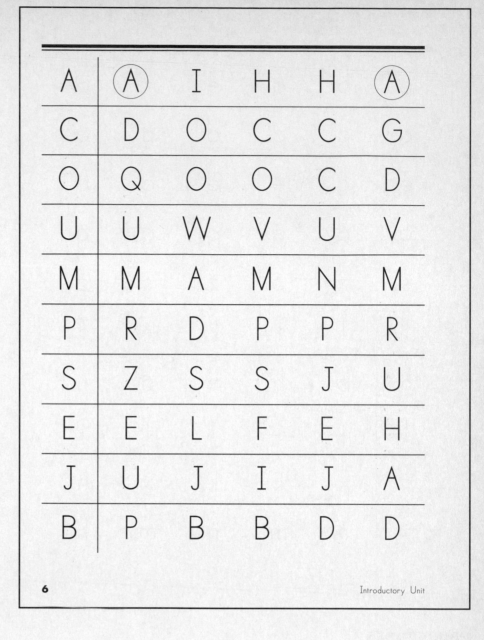

PROCEDURES

Ask volunteers to read the lines of letters aloud. Demonstrate the first item on the board or overhead projector. Indicate the letter **A**, then find and circle the two matching letters in the line to the right. Have the students complete the exercise independently. Correct the exercise on the board or overhead projector. Check each student's work and provide immediate feedback.

Teaching Note: You may want to prepare similar pages with other letters for additional reinforcement.

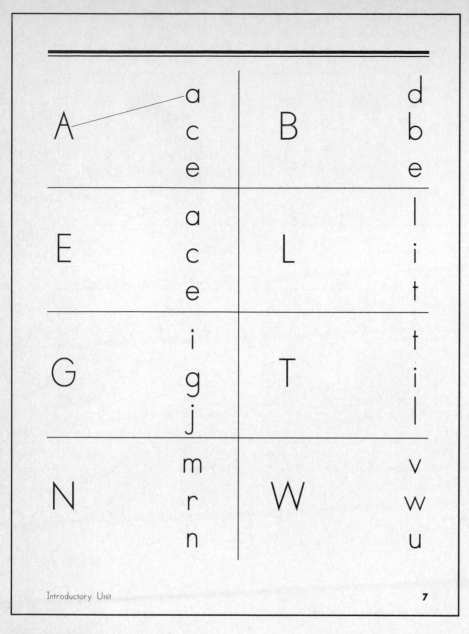

PROCEDURES

Copy the first item on the board or overhead projector. Read the letters aloud. Demonstrate the first item by drawing a line between capital **A** and lower-case **a**. Have students complete the exercise independently. Correct the exercise on the board or overhead projector. Then check each student's work and provide immediate feedback.

Teaching Note: You may want to prepare similar pages with other letters for additional reinforcement.

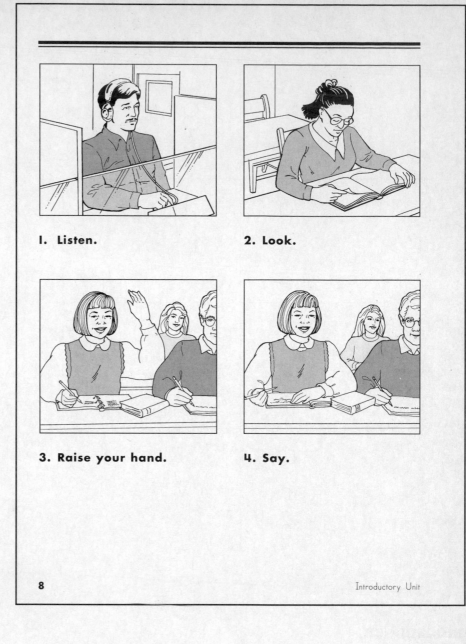

1. **Listen.**   2. **Look.**

3. **Raise your hand.**   4. **Say.**

8   Introductory Unit

PROCEDURES

Read each direction line aloud.
Have students repeat. Use the illustration on the page and pantomime
to demonstrate meaning. Then say
the direction line and have students
act it out. When you have taught all
the direction lines, say them in and
out of order and have students act
them out.

Teaching Note: During the teaching
of individual units, have students
refer back to these pages whenever
necessary.

5. Circle.

6. Underline.

7. Write.

8. Work with a partner.

Introductory Unit   9

PROCEDURES

Follow the instructions on page 8.

Teaching Note: Duplicate as needed to provide students with writing paper for extra practice in writing letters, numbers, words and sentences.

Introductory Unit

Unit 1

Personal Communication

Look at the picture.

Where are the people?

What are they doing?

II

UNIT COMPETENCIES

1. Ask for and give personal information
2. Complete a simple form
3. Introduce yourself

Unit 1 Optional Materials

● Alphabet cards for letters **n, l, a, c,** and **t.** Number cards for **0** through **10;** picture cards showing numbers of objects from zero to ten.

● Word cards for **name, first name, last name, address, number, street, city, state, zip code,** and **telephone number.** Name cards with your first name and last name on them and name cards for each student.

● Realia: a picture of your, or another, family; an envelope that was mailed to you; a real telephone; and a telephone directory.

♦ Blackline Master 1: Identification Form, page 142 and Blackline Master 2: Telephone, page 143.

Teaching Note

Use pages 8 and 9 of the Introductory Unit to clarify the direction lines in this unit.

COMPETENCIES (page 11)

Ask for and give personal information

Introduce yourself

PREPARATION

Begin the class by introducing yourself and having students introduce themselves to you and each other. If necessary, teach them how to ask other people's names and tell other people their own names. Follow these suggestions.

● Hold up the card with your name on it. Say, *My name is (name).* Have students repeat with their names.

● Have a volunteer come forward. Ask, *What's your name?* Help the student answer. Hold up the stu-

dent's name card and read it aloud. Give the name card to the student. Repeat with each student.

PRESENTATION

Teaching Note: Use this page to warm up students, to check and draw on prior knowledge, and to spark interest.

Have students open their books to page 11. Read the unit title and the questions aloud. Students may be able to name a few objects in the picture, but you will probably have to prompt them by naming items and having students repeat.

FOLLOW-UP

Learning Each Other's Names: Have

the class sit in a circle. Ask the person beside you to say his or her name aloud. Then say, *My name is (name), and this is (name of person beside you).* Each person, in turn, says his or her own name and tries to recall and say the names of the people who have already given their names.

♦ Have students change seats and repeat the game.

Ask for and give personal
information

Introduce yourself

Name

▭ **I. Listen and practice the dialog.**

What's your name?

Nancy.

▭ **2. Your teacher writes your name.**

Name: _____

You write your name.

Name: _____

Name: _____

Name: _____

Name: _____

Name: _____

Name: _____

▭ **3. Listen for** name. **Raise your hand.**

12   Unit I

PREPARATION

Preteach the new language in the lesson. Follow these suggestions.

● Review introductions. Follow the instructions on page 11.

● Introduce the word card for **name.** Hold up the card, read it, and have students repeat the word. Call attention to the initial letter of the word. See "Presenting Recognition Words" on page vii.

● Say, *What is your name?* and hold up the word card for **name.** Prompt a volunteer to say his or her name and to hold up the card with his or her name on it. Repeat with other students.

Teaching Note: Throughout the unit, if students do not want to give out personal information, such as their addresses or telephone numbers, they may use fictitious information instead.

PRESENTATION

1. Focus attention on the illustration. Have students say as much as they can about it. You may want to cue them by indicating items or saying names of items and having students indicate them. Restate their ideas in acceptable English and write them on the board or overhead projector. Identify the Asian woman as Nancy. Write her name on the board.

Present the dialog. See "Presenting Dialogs" on page vii.

2. Help students read the directions. Demonstrate on the board or overhead projector by filling in the blank with your name. Write each student's name in the appropriate space in his or her book. Then have students complete the exercise independently. Check each student's work and provide feedback as needed.

3. Help students read the directions. Then, present the listening. See "Presenting Listenings" on page vii. Make sure students respond correctly. Have students listen again so they have additional opportunities to hear and respond.

4. Help students read the directions. Demonstrate by circling **Name** on

12   Real-Life English

4. Circle Name **and** NAME.

Application

(Name): _Lee_   _Nancy_
      Last   First

ID CARD APPLICATION

(NAME): _____
     LAST   FIRST

5. Say the letters. Write the letters.

N n _____

N n

6. Write n. **Write your name. Say the sentence.**

My _n_ame is _____ .

My ___ame is _____ .

My ___ame is _____ .

My ___ame is _____ .

Unit 1   **13**

---

the board or overhead projector. Then have students complete the exercise in pairs. Correct the exercise on the board or overhead projector.

5. Present or review the letter **n.** See "Presenting Letters" on page vii. Then have students complete the exercise. Check students' work. For extra reinforcement, use pages 3 and 10 of the Introductory Unit.

6. Help students read the directions. Demonstrate by completing the first item on the board or overhead projector. Then ask students to complete the exercise independently. Have them check their work in pairs and say their sentences aloud to each other and then to the class.

FOLLOW-UP

Names, Names, Names: Give each student his or her name card. Then arrange students in groups of four or five. Join a group to demonstrate the activity. First have group members state their names and display their name cards. Then with cards still visible, repeat all the names in the group. Have students take turns naming all the members of the group. Then have all groups complete the activity. Finally, ask a volunteer from each group to name the members of his or her group for the class.

♦ Have students place their name cards in a pile in the center of the group. Then have a student match people and their name cards. Repeat with different students doing the matching.

Introduce yourself

Complete a simple form

First Name   Last Name

🔲 **1. Listen and practice the dialog.**

➤ What's your first name?
● Nancy.
➤ What's your last name?
● Lee.

2. Your teacher writes your name.

Name: _____   _____
        First   Last

You write your name.

Name: _____   _____
        First   Last

Name: _____   _____
        First   Last

🔲 **3. Listen. Circle the word you hear.**

a. first   (last)

b. (name)   first

c. first   (last)

14   Unit 1

PREPARATION

Preteach the new language in the lesson. Follow these suggestions.

● To teach **first name** and **last name,** show a picture of your, or another, family. (Or draw stick figures on the board to represent a family.) Identify everyone by saying, *His (her) name is (first and last name).* Say, *My last name is (last name).* Then say the last name of each of the family members in the picture or drawing. Point to each and say, *His (her) last name is (last name).* Repeat with first names. Ask volunteers to tell you their first and last names.

● Present or review the recognition words **first name** and **last name.** First, hold up the word card for **first name** and say, *My first name is (first*

name). Repeat with your last name. Have students repeat the target words. Call attention to the first letters in the words on the cards. Then hold up cards at random and have the whole class, and then volunteers, read the cards aloud. Continue until the class can do this easily.

PRESENTATION

1. Focus attention on the illustration. Have students say as much as they can about it. You may want to cue them by indicating items or saying names of items and having students indicate them. Identify Nancy Lee. Ask, *What's her first name? What's her last name?* Repeat their ideas in acceptable English, and write them on the board or overhead projector.

Present the dialog. See "Presenting Dialogs" on page vii.

2. Help students read the directions. Demonstrate by completing the first item on the board or overhead projector. Write each student's first name and last name in his or her book. Have students complete the exercise independently. Check each student's work and provide feedback as necessary.

3. Help students read the directions. Then, present the listening. See "Presenting Listenings" on page vii. Correct students' work. Ask volunteers to read the correct answers aloud.

4. Help students read the directions. Demonstrate by circling the first item on the board or overhead pro-

---

14   Real-Life English

4. Circle Last, LAST, First, **and** FIRST.

Application
Name : _____
(Last)   (First)

ID CARD APPLICATION
NAME : _____
(LAST)   (FIRST)

About You **5. Write your name in 4.**

6. Say the letters. Write the letters.

L l

L l

About You **7. Write l. Write your last name. Say the sentence.**

My l ast name is _____ .

My __ ast name is _____ .

My __ ast name is _____ .

jector. Then have students complete the exercise independently. Check students' work. Then copy the form on the board or the overhead projector and have volunteers circle the answers.

About You **5.** Help students read the directions. Demonstrate by completing the form on the board or overhead projector. Then have students work in pairs to help each other complete the exercise. Ask students to check their work by referring to their name cards. Check students' work.

6. Present or review the letter **l.** See "Presenting Letters" on page vii. Then have students complete the exercise. Check students' work. For extra reinforcement, use pages 2 and 10 of the Introductory Unit.

About You **7.** Help students read the directions. Demonstrate by completing the first item on the board or overhead projector. Then have students complete the exercise independently. Have students check their work in pairs and say their sentences aloud to each other and then to the class.

FOLLOW-UP

First Names First: Have students bring in pictures of one or more people in their families or of one of two others they know. Or have them draw stick figures of themselves and one other person. Then have students select partners and tell the first names and last names of the people in the pictures or drawings. Have students change partners and repeat the activity. Circulate among them and offer help as needed. Ask volunteers to show their pictures to the class and tell the class the first and last names of the people.

♦ Have students write the first and last names of each person under the stick figures.

Complete a simple form

Ask for and give personal
information

Address   Number   Street

🔲 **1. Listen and practice the dialog.**

What's your address?   22 Pine Street.

📋 **2. Your teacher writes your address.**

Address: _____
         Number   Street

You write your address.

Address: _____
         Number   Street

Address: _____
         Number   Street

Address: _____
         Number   Street

🔲 **3. Listen. Circle the word you hear.**

a. (address)   number   street

b. address   (number)   street

c. address   number   (street)

PREPARATION

Preteach the new language in the lesson. Follow these suggestions.

● Preteach or review the numerals **0** to **10**. Follow the instructions on page 4.

● To preteach **address, number,** and **street,** write your own, or the school's, number and street on the board or overhead projector. Show a realia envelope with the same address. Say, *This is (my) address.* Point to the number on the board or screen and on the envelope and say, *This is the number.* Repeat for the street.

● One by one, introduce the word cards for **address, number,** and **street.** Say each word as you indicate

the corresponding part of the address on the board or overhead projector. Have students repeat. Call attention to the initial letters. Then, one at a time, hold up word cards and have individuals indicate the corresponding portion of the address on the board. Repeat until students can identify the number and the street easily.

PRESENTATION

1. Focus attention on the illustration. Help students read the speech balloons. Have students say as much as they can about the illustration. You may want to cue them by indicating items or by saying names of items and having students indicate them. Restate their ideas in acceptable

English and write them on the board or overhead projector.

Present the dialog. See "Presenting Dialogs" on page vii.

📋 **2.** Present or review writing numerals **0** through **10**. Use pages 4 and 10 of the Introductory Unit. Help students read the directions. Demonstrate by completing the first item on the board. Write each student's address in his or her book. Have students do the exercise independently. Check students' work and provide feedback as necessary.

3. Help students read the directions. Then, present the listening. See "Presenting Listenings" on page vii. Correct students' work. Ask volunteers to read the correct answers

4. **Circle** ADDRESS, Number, **and** Street.

🎓 Monterey College Registration

NAME: *Hall* *James*
Last First

(ADDRESS): *22* *Pine* (Street)
(Number) (Street)

5. **Say the letters. Write the letters.**

A a

A a

6. **Write** A. **Write your address. Say your address.**

About You

A ddress: _____
Number Street

___ ddress: _____
Number Street

7. **Write your name and address.**

About You

🍎 OAKLAND ADULT LEARNING CENTER

NAME: _____
Last First

ADDRESS: _____
Number Street

aloud.

4. Help students read the directions. Demonstrate by completing the first item on the board or overhead projector. Then have students complete the exercise independently. Correct the exercise on the board or overhead projector.

5. Present or review the letter **a.** See "Presenting Letters" on page vii. Then have students complete the exercise. Check students' work. For extra reinforcement, use pages 2 and 10 of the Introductory Unit.

About You **6.** Help students read the directions. Demonstrate by completing the first item on the board or overhead projector. Have students

complete the exercise independently. Check students' work. Then have volunteers read their answers to the class.

About You **7.** Help students read the directions and the words on the form. Demonstrate by completing the items on the board. Then have students complete the exercise independently. Check students' work and provide feedback as needed.

FOLLOW-UP

What's Your Address? Ask several students to write their names and addresses on the board. Say words and phrases from the unit, such as **first name** or **street.** Have the students point to the corresponding words or numbers on the board.

Repeat the activity with several different students.

♦ Have students fold a sheet of paper in half, then in half again the other way to form four boxes. Instruct students to ask four different classmates their names and addresses. Classmates respond by writing the information in the boxes.

Complete a simple form

Ask for and give personal
information

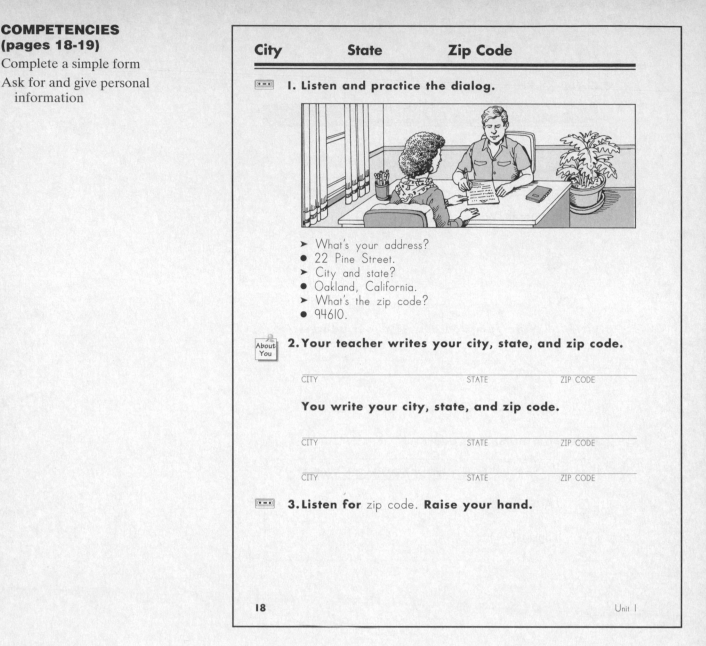

City　　　State　　　Zip Code

1. Listen and practice the dialog.

> ➤ What's your address?
> ● 22 Pine Street.
> ➤ City and state?
> ● Oakland, California.
> ➤ What's the zip code?
> ● 94610.

2. Your teacher writes your city, state, and zip code.

_____
CITY　　　　　　　　　　　STATE　　　　　ZIP CODE

You write your city, state, and zip code.

_____
CITY　　　　　　　　　　　STATE　　　　　ZIP CODE

_____
CITY　　　　　　　　　　　STATE　　　　　ZIP CODE

3. Listen for zip code. **Raise your hand.**

18　　　　　　　　　　　　　　　　　　　Unit 1

PREPARATION

Preteach the new language in the
lesson. Follow these suggestions.

● Write the school's city and state on
the board or overhead projector.
Say, *(I) live in (city and state).*

● Show students an envelope mailed
to you. Point out the zip code and
explain that it is an important part of
a mailing address. Add the zip code
to the school's address on the board
or overhead projector. If your students live in different cities or have
different zip codes, write these on
the board or overhead projector as
well. Indicate parts of the addresses
and have volunteers tell you if they
are the city, state, or zip code.

● One at a time, hold up word cards
for **city, state,** and **zip code.** Say the

words and have students repeat. Call
attention to the initial consonant in
each word. Hold up one of the word
cards, have a volunteer read it, and
indicate the appropriate item in your
school's address on the board or
overhead projector. Continue until
students can do this easily.

Teaching Note: Explain that zip
codes are usually read one number at
a time. Tell students that the numeral **0** is usually pronounced like the
letter **o.**

PRESENTATION

1. Focus attention on the illustration.
Have students say as much as they
can about it. You may wish to cue
them by indicating items or saying
names of items and having students

indicate them. Restate their ideas in
acceptable English and write them
on the board or overhead projector.

Present the dialog. See "Presenting
Dialogs" on page vii.

2. Help students read the directions. Demonstrate by completing the first item on the board. Write
each student's city, state, and zip
code in his or her book. Have students complete the exercise independently. Check students' work and
provide any feedback necessary.

3. Help students read the directions.
Then, present the listening. See
"Presenting Listenings" on page vii.
Make sure students respond correctly. Have students listen again so they
have additional opportunities to hear
and respond.

4. Circle City, State, **and** Zip Code.

ADDRESS : _22_   _Pine Street_
          Number   Street

          Oakland   _California_   _94610_
          (City)   (State)   (Zip Code)

5. Say the letters. Write the letters.

C c _____

C c _____

[About You] **6. Write** c. **Write your** zip code. **Say the sentence.**

My zip _c_ode is _____.

My zip ___ode is _____.

My zip ___ode is _____.

[About You] **7. Write your** city, state, **and** zip code.

ADDRESS : _____
          NUMBER   STREET

          _____
          CITY   STATE   ZIP CODE

Teaching Note: Make additional word cards to present identification numbers your students need to provide, such as Social Security numbers, driver's license numbers, etc.

4. Help students read the directions. Demonstrate by circling **City** on the board or overhead projector. Have students complete the exercise independently. Correct the exercise on the board or overhead projector.

5. Present the letter **c.** See "Presenting Letters" on page vii. Then have students complete the activity. For extra reinforcement, use pages 2 and 10 of the Introductory Unit.

[About You] **6.** Help students read the directions. Demonstrate by completing the first item on the board or overhead projector. Then have students complete the exercise independently. Check students' work. Then ask volunteers to read their sentences to the class.

[About You] **7.** Help students read the directions. Demonstrate by filling in the form on the board or overhead projector. Then have students work in pairs to help each other complete the exercise. Ask volunteers to read their answers aloud.

FOLLOW-UP

Interviews: Have pairs of students interview each other. First demonstrate the activity with a partner. Ask, *What's your address? What's your city? What's your state? What's your zip code?* To help students remember the questions, write the words **address, city, state,** and **zip code** on the board or overhead projector. Then have students do the activity. Circulate among them to offer help as needed.

♦ Provide each student with an envelope. Have pairs of students address their envelopes to each other.

Complete a simple form

Ask for and give personal
information

Telephone Number

🔲 **1. Listen and practice the dialog.**

What's your telephone number?

(503) 555-6311.

About You **2. Your teacher writes your telephone number.**

Telephone Number: _____

You write your telephone number.

Telephone Number: _____

Telephone Number: _____

Telephone Number: _____

🔲 **3. Listen for** telephone number. **Raise your hand.**

20   Unit 1

PREPARATION

Preteach the new language in the
lesson. Follow these suggestions.

● Review numerals from **0** through
10. Follow the instructions on page 4.

● Show students a real telephone or
Blackline Master 2: Telephone.
Indicate the numerals on the phone
and have students say the numbers
as you point to them.

● Write the school's telephone number on the board or overhead projector. Say, *This is the school's telephone number.* Ask volunteers to say
their telephone numbers.

● Hold up the word card for
Telephone Number, read the words,
and have students repeat them. Call
attention to the initial consonant in

each word. Hold up the word card
again and ask a volunteer to write his
or her telephone number on the
board or overhead projector.

PRESENTATION

1. Focus attention on the illustration.
Help students read the speech balloons. Have them say as much as
they can about the illustration. You
may wish to cue them by indicating
items or saying names of objects and
having students indicate them. Help
them identify the people. Restate
their ideas in acceptable English and
write them on the board or overhead
projector.

Present the dialog. See "Presenting
Dialogs" on page vii.

About You **2.** Help students read the
directions. Demonstrate by filling in your telephone number on the
board or overhead projector. Write
each student's telephone number in
his or her book. Have students
complete the exercise independently.
Check students' work.

3. Help students read the directions.
Then, present the listening. See
"Presenting Listenings" on page vii.
Make sure students respond correctly. Have students listen again so they
have additional opportunities to hear
and respond.

4. Help students read the directions.
Demonstrate by circling **Telephone
Number** on the board or overhead
projector. Then have students complete the exercise independently.

4. Circle Telephone Number.

```
╭─────────────── • REGISTRATION CARD • ───────────────╮
│ Name:                        │ Address:                │
│ Williams      Harold         │ 35  Riverside Drive      │
│ Last          First          │ Number     Street        │
│ (Telephone Number):          │ Oakland  California  94610│
│ (510) 555-6311               │ City      State    Zip Code│
╰──────────────────────────────┴──────────────────────────╯
```

5. Say the letters. Write the letters.

T t

T t

About You
6. Write t. **Write your telephone number.**
Say the sentence.

My __t__elephone number is _____.

My ___elephone number is _____.

My ___elephone number is _____.

About You
7. Complete the form.

```
╭─────────────── • REGISTRATION CARD • ───────────────╮
│ Name:                        │ Address:                │
│                              │                          │
│ Last          First          │ Number     Street        │
│ Telephone Number:            │                          │
│                              │ City      State    Zip Code│
╰──────────────────────────────┴──────────────────────────╯
```

Unit I   **21**

Check students' work.

5. Present the letter **t.** See "Presenting Letters" on page vii. Then have students complete the activity. For extra reinforcement, use pages 3 and 10 of the Introductory Unit.

About You **6.** Help students read the directions. Demonstrate by completing the first item on the board or overhead projector. Have students complete the exercise independently. Have volunteers say their sentences to the class.

About You **7.** Help students read the directions. Demonstrate by completing the form on the board or overhead projector. Then have students complete the activity. Ask volunteers to read their answers aloud.

Teaching Note: Teach students to say **Hello** when answering the telephone and to say **Good-by** at the end of the conversation.

FOLLOW-UP

Important Telephone Numbers: Ask students what important telephone numbers they need. Look them up in the telephone book for the students and write them on the board or overhead projector. Read the numbers aloud with the class. Have students copy the numbers they need.

♦ Have pairs of students exchange telephone numbers and then pantomime calling each other. First, model the activity with a volunteer. Say the number you are calling aloud as you pantomime dialing on a copy

of Blackline Master 2: Telephone. Prompt your partner to say **Hello.** Ask, *Is this (first name)?* Then have students do the activity. Have students change partners and repeat the activity.

PRESENTATION

On the board or overhead projector, draw a grid similar to the one in the book.

Help students read the directions. Demonstrate by filling in your name and telephone number in the grid you drew.

Instruct students to circulate around the room and have their classmates write their names and telephone numbers on the grid in their books. Assist as needed. As students circulate, have each take time to write his or her name and telephone number in the grid on the board or overhead projector. Use the list on the board or overhead projector to check students' lists to make sure they're complete.

FOLLOW-UP

Call a Friend: Use the class telephone lists students just made. Have a volunteer come forward and pantomime calling a classmate on the telephone by saying his or her telephone number aloud. Ask the student who hears his or her number to come forward and pantomime answering the telephone. Suggest that the answerer ask for the telephone number of another student in the class. Repeat until all who want to participate have had a turn.

♦ Write each student's telephone number on a slip of paper. Give one slip to each student. Have students circulate around the room to find the person with that telephone number. Model the question, *Is your tele-* *phone number (555-4801)?* Have students tell the class who their numbers belong to, *(Manuel's) telephone number is (555-4801).*

Complete the form.

CITY LEARNING CENTER

NAME _____
       LAST   FIRST

TELEPHONE NUMBER (____) _____

ADDRESS _____
         NUMBER   STREET

_____
CITY   STATE   ZIP CODE

Unit 1   **23**

PREPARATION

Briefly review the new language before students open their books. Duplicate a copy of Blackline Master 1: Identification Form for each student and have them complete it. Check the information carefully and provide specific help as needed until you are sure students feel confident that they know all the words.

PRESENTATION

Use any of the procedures in "Evaluation," page viii, with these pages. Record individuals' results on the Unit 1 Individual Competency Chart. Record the class's results on the Class Cumulative Competency Chart.

ENGLISH IN ACTION

An Optional Cooperative Learning Activity: Have students work together to create a master class telephone list in alphabetical order. Duplicate a copy of the list for every student.

Circle the word.

1. NAME   N A (N A M E) N E

2. NAME   M A N E (N A M E)

3. NAME   N E (N A M E) M E

4. FIRST   F I R (F I R S T)

5. FIRST   F (F I R S T) T F

6. FIRST   S T (F I R S T) F

7. LAST   L A (L A S T) L A

8. LAST   L (L A S T) T L A

9. LAST   L A S (L A S T) L

PRESENTATION

Help students read the directions. Model the word search puzzle activity by writing **NANAMENE** on the board in letters approximately the same size as those on the word card for **NAME.** Hold the word card against the first four letters on the board, shake your head, and say, *No.* Move the card so it lines up with **ANAM** and repeat your rejection of the match. Move the card again so that it lines up with **NAME.** This time indicate your acceptance of the match and circle the word.

Have students complete the activity in pairs. Circulate among them to offer help as necessary.

Copy the word search puzzle on the board or overhead projector. Have volunteers come forward one at a time to circle the correct answer for each item.

FOLLOW-UP

Have students work in pairs to devise word searches for the words **address, number, street,** and **telephone.** Have them exchange their word searches with another pair of students and work out the answers.

Unit

2 Our Community

Look at the picture.

Where are the people?

What are they doing?

25

Unit 2 Overview

UNIT COMPETENCIES

1. Identify places
2. Say where places are
3. Buy stamps and mail letters
4. Understand emergency words
5. Report emergencies by telephone

Unit 2 Optional Materials

● Alphabet cards for letters **h, p, o, s,** and **f.** Number cards for numerals **0** through **20;** picture cards showing numbers of objects from zero to twenty.

● Picture cards and word cards of places in a community (fire department, school, post office, mailbox, bank, police station, hospital) and of emergency words (fire, accident, ambulance).

● Realia: a large map of your community with places presented in the unit labeled, postage stamps and a telephone directory.

♦ Blackline Master 2: Telephone, page 143.

Teaching Note

Use pages 8 and 9 of the Introductory Unit to clarify the direction lines in this unit.

COMPETENCIES (page 25)

Identify places

PRESENTATION

Teaching Note: Use this page to warm up students, to check and draw on their prior knowledge, and to spark interest.

Have students open their books to page 25. Read the unit title and the questions aloud. Encourage students to identify as many items in the picture as they can and to describe what is happening. As students may be able to say very little, you might have to prompt them by indicating items for them to name or by saying names of items and having students indicate them. Model any words students do not know.

You might mention places in your community, such as the hospital or post office, and ask students to raise their hands if they have seen them or been inside them.

FOLLOW-UP

Magazine Pictures

Provide pairs of students with magazines that have pictures of community scenes. Ask students to cut out pictures that include the objects they saw on page 25, such as a car or a public telephone. Have each pair of students show their pictures to the class and say the names of one or more of the objects in the pictures. Provide feedback as necessary.

♦ Have pairs of students join together to make groups of four. Ask each pair to show its pictures to the other pair and name as many objects as they can for them. Circulate among students to offer help as needed.

Identify places

Say where places are

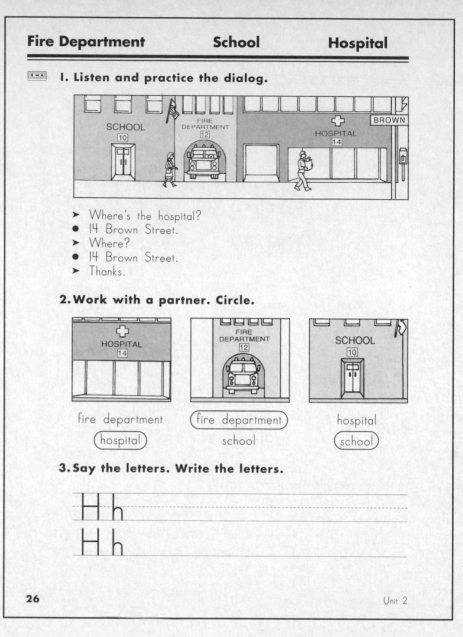

Fire Department   School   Hospital

🔲 **I. Listen and practice the dialog.**

➤ Where's the hospital?
● 14 Brown Street.
➤ Where?
● 14 Brown Street.
➤ Thanks.

2. Work with a partner. Circle.

fire department
(hospital)

(fire department)
school

hospital
(school)

3. Say the letters. Write the letters.

H h

H h

26   Unit 2

PREPARATION

Preteach the new language in the lesson. Follow these suggestions.

● Use picture cards and word cards to preteach the recognition words **fire department, hospital,** and **school.** See "Presenting Recognition Words" on page vii.

● Preteach or review numerals **0** to **10.** For extra reinforcement, use pages 4 and 10 of the Introductory Unit.

● Review the phrase **telephone number,** if necessary. See page 20 of Unit 1.

● Preteach the dialog. Focus attention on the large map you made. Pantomime looking for a place on the map. Model the question,

Where's the (hospital)? Have students repeat. Then model the answer, *(14 Brown Street),* and have students repeat.

PRESENTATION

1. Focus attention on the illustration. Help students identify buildings and read the signs. Have them say as much as they can about the illustration. You may want to cue students by indicating items for them to name or by saying names of items and having students indicate them. Restate students' ideas in acceptable English and write them on the board or overhead projector.

Present the dialog. See "Presenting Dialogs" on page vii.

2. Help students read the directions. Demonstrate by completing the first item on the board or overhead projector. Then have students complete the exercise in pairs. Correct the exercise on the board or overhead projector.

3. Present or review the letter **h.** See "Presenting Letters" on page vii. Then have students complete the activity. For extra review or reinforcement, use pages 2 and 10 of the Introductory Unit.

4. Help students read the directions. Demonstrate by completing the first item on the board or overhead projector. Then have students complete the exercise independently. Then check everyone's work by copying the chart on the board or overhead

4. Circle Fire Department **and** Hospital.
Underline the telephone numbers.

IMPORTANT ☎ NUMBERS

🔥	(Fire Department)	911
✚	(Hospital)	555-0121
	School	555-1000

5. Write h. **Say the words.**

_h_ ospital   ___ospital   ___ospital

_h_ ospital   ___ospital   ___ospital

sc _h_ ool   sc ___ool   sc ___ool

sc _h_ ool   sc ___ool   sc ___ool

About You **6. Work with a partner. Complete the chart.**

IMPORTANT ☎ NUMBERS

Fire Department	
Hospital	
School	

projector and having volunteers come forward, one at a time, to complete the items.

5. Help students read the directions. Demonstrate by completing the first item on the board or overhead projector. Then have students complete the exercise independently. Check students' work. Then ask volunteers to read the words aloud and match them to picture cards.

About You **6.** Help students read the directions. Then have students complete the exercise in pairs. Ask volunteers to read the answers aloud.

Teaching Note: Students may need help finding the telephone numbers of the places mentioned in this unit. Look up the numbers in a telephone directory as students watch. Write the numbers on the board or overhead projector. If 911 is not the number for a fire in your area, write your community's emergency fire number on the board for students to copy. You may wish to point out where in the phone book students can learn which emergencies they can use 911 for, and what number(s) to call if 911 is not available in your area. Have students use Blackline Master 2: Telephone to practice dialing 911.

FOLLOW-UP

Giving Directions: Draw attention to the large community map you made. Have students work in pairs to use the dialog on the page to ask and answer questions about the location of the buildings on the map.

Circulate to offer help as needed.

♦ Have volunteers come forward to ask the class for the locations of buildings on the map. As students answer, have the volunteer find the building and point to it.

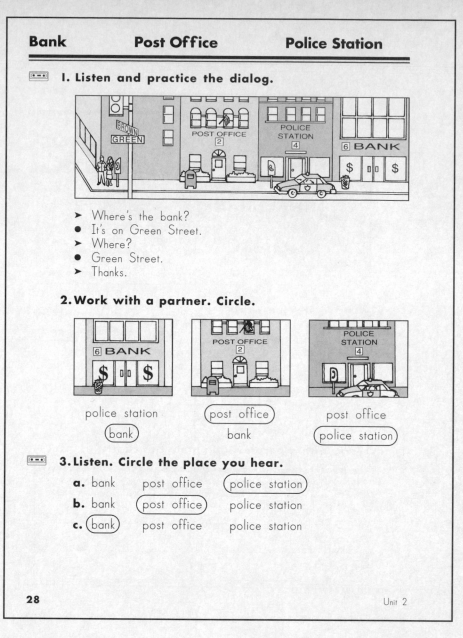

Bank   Post Office   Police Station

1. Listen and practice the dialog.

➤ Where's the bank?
● It's on Green Street.
➤ Where?
● Green Street.
➤ Thanks.

2. Work with a partner. Circle.

police station
(bank)

(post office)
bank

post office
(police station)

3. Listen. Circle the place you hear.

a. bank   post office   (police station)

b. bank   (post office)   police station

c. (bank)   post office   police station

28   Unit 2

PREPARATION

Preteach the new language in the lesson. Follow these suggestions.

● Use picture cards and word cards to preteach the recognition words **bank, post office,** and **police station.** See "Presenting Recognition Words" on page vii.

● Preteach the dialog. Focus attention on the large map you made. Model the question, *Where's the (bank)?* Have students repeat. Then model the answer, *(It's on Green Street),* and have students repeat.

PRESENTATION

1. Focus attention on the illustration. Help students identify the buildings and read the street signs. Have them say as much as they can about the illustration. You may want to cue students by indicating items for them to name or by saying names of items and having students indicate them. Restate students' ideas in acceptable English and write them on the board or overhead projector.

Present the dialog. See "Presenting Dialogs" on page vii.

2. Help students read the directions. Demonstrate by circling the first item on the board or overhead projector. Then have students complete the exercise in pairs. Have volunteers say their answers aloud.

3. Help students read the directions. Then, present the listening. See "Presenting Listenings" on page vii. Correct students' work. Ask volun-teers to read the correct answers aloud.

4. Present or review the letters **p** and **o.** See "Presenting Letters" on page vii. Then have students complete the activity on the page. For extra review or reinforcement, use pages 3 and 10 of the Introductory Unit.

5. Help students read the directions. Demonstrate by completing the first item on the board or overhead projector. Then have students complete the exercise independently. Check students' work. Then ask volunteers to say the words aloud and match them to picture cards.

About You **6.** Help students read the direc-tions. Demonstrate by complet-ing the first item on the board or overhead projector. Then have stu-

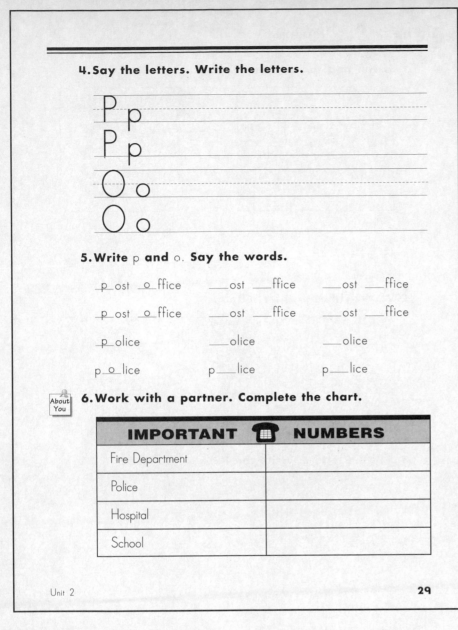

4. Say the letters. Write the letters.

P p

P p

O o

O o

5. Write p and o. Say the words.

_p_ ost _o_ ffice	___ost ___ffice	___ost ___ffice
_p_ ost _o_ ffice	___ost ___ffice	___ost ___ffice
_p_ olice	___olice	___olice
p _o_ lice	p ___lice	p ___lice

About You

6. Work with a partner. Complete the chart.

IMPORTANT ☏ NUMBERS	
Fire Department	
Police	
Hospital	
School	

Unit 2   **29**

dents work in pairs to complete the activity. Ask volunteers to read their answers aloud.

location of these places and find them on their own maps.

FOLLOW-UP

Locating Places: Call attention to the large community map you made. Ask volunteers to come forward and locate the police station, post office, and bank(s). Then have students work in pairs to ask and answer questions about where these places are located in your community. Circulate to offer help as needed.

♦ Distribute copies of a map of your community's downtown area. Have pairs of students locate important places in your community. Ask them to name the places they've found. Then have their classmates ask the

Buy stamps and mail letters

Say where places are

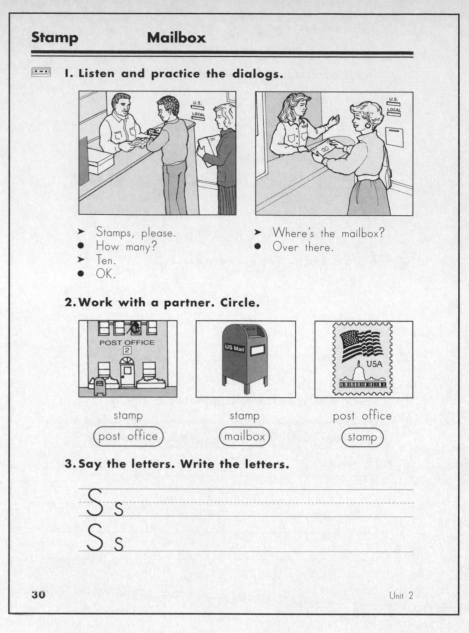

PREPARATION

Preteach the new language in the lesson. Follow these suggestions.

● Use realia, picture cards, and word cards to preteach the recognition words **stamp** and **mailbox.** See "Presenting Recognition Words" on page vii.

● Preteach or review numerals **0** to **20.** For extra reinforcement, use pages 4 and 10 of the Introductory Unit.

● Preteach the dialogs. First, teach the phrase **How many?** Hold up some pencils, say, *How many? One? Two? Four?* and show students the corresponding number of pencils. Repeat with other objects. Then give a volunteer several stamps. Say,

Stamps, please. Prompt the volunteer to ask, *How many?* Specify a number and help the volunteer give that many stamps to you.

To teach the phrase **Over there,** put the picture card of the mailbox on the other side of the room. Ask, *Where's the mailbox?* Have students repeat. Point to the picture card of the mailbox, answer, *Over there,* and have students repeat.

PRESENTATION

1. Focus attention on the illustration. Help students identify the people and places. Have them say as much as they can about the illustration. You may want to cue students by indicating items for them to name or by saying names of items and having

students indicate them. Restate students' ideas in acceptable English and write them on the board or overhead projector.

Present each dialog in turn. See "Presenting Dialogs" on page vii.

Teaching Note: You may want to tell students the current price for a first-class stamp. Help students figure out how much ten stamps cost.

2. Help students read the directions. Demonstrate by circling the first item on the board or overhead projector. Then have them complete the exercise in pairs. Correct the activity on the board or overhead projector.

3. Present or review the letter **s.** See "Presenting Letters" on page vii. Then have students complete the

4. Write s, p, **and** o. **Say the words.**

_s_ tam _p_   ___ tam ___   ___ tam ___   ___ tam ___

mailb _o_ x   mailb ___ x   mailb ___ x   mailb ___ x

5. Listen. Circle the word you hear.

a. (post office)   stamp

b. (stamps)   mailbox

c. (mailbox)   stamp

6. Write your name and address on the lines.
Circle stamp.

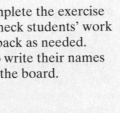

Name _____

Address _____
NUMBER   STREET

_____
CITY   STATE   ZIP CODE

Place (stamp) here

River City Bank

6 Green Street

River City, CA 98731

activity. For extra review or reinforcement, use pages 3 and 10 of the Introductory Unit.

4. Help students read the directions. Demonstrate by completing the first item on the board or overhead projector. Then have students complete the exercise independently. Check students' work. Then ask volunteers to read the words aloud and match them to picture cards.

5. Help students read the directions. Then, present the listening. See "Presenting Listenings" on page vii. Correct students' work. Ask volunteers to read the correct answers aloud.

6. Help students read the directions. Demonstrate by completing the exercise on the board. Then

have students complete the exercise independently. Check students' work and provide feedback as needed. Ask volunteers to write their names and addresses on the board.

FOLLOW-UP

At the Post Office: Play the role of a postal worker and have a student play the role of a customer. Use realia stamps. Prompt the student to ask you for stamps. Say, *How many?* When the student tells you, give him or her the appropriate number. Repeat with other students. Then ask a student to take over your role as postal worker. As an extension of this activity, you might arrange a trip to the post office.

♦ Have students do the role-play in pairs, taking turns as postal worker and customer. Circulate to offer help as needed. Have volunteers present their dialogs to the class.

Understand emergency words

Report emergencies by telephone

Say where places are

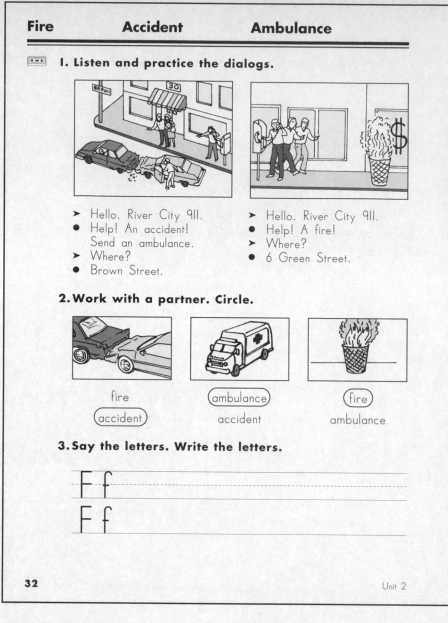

Fire   Accident   Ambulance

1. Listen and practice the dialogs.

➤ Hello. River City 911.
● Help! An accident!
  Send an ambulance.
➤ Where?
● Brown Street.

➤ Hello. River City 911.
● Help! A fire!
➤ Where?
● 6 Green Street.

2. Work with a partner. Circle.

fire
(accident)

(ambulance)
accident

(fire)
ambulance

3. Say the letters. Write the letters.

F f

F f

32   Unit 2

PREPARATION

Preteach the new language in the lesson. Follow these suggestions.

● Use picture cards and word cards to preteach the recognition words **fire, accident,** and **ambulance.** See "Presenting Recognition Words" on page vii.

● Preteach the dialogs. To teach the word **help,** pantomime tripping and hurting your back. Then say, *Help!* Have students repeat the word. To teach **send,** put the picture of the accident at one end of the chalk rail. Place the picture card of the ambulance at the other end of the chalk rail. Say, *Help! An accident! Send an ambulance,* and push the picture card of the ambulance along the chalk rail to the picture of the accident.

PRESENTATION

1. Focus attention on the illustration. Help students describe what's happening. Have them say as much as they can about the illustration. You may want to cue students by indicating items for them to name or by saying names of items and having students indicate them. Restate students' ideas in acceptable English and write them on the board or overhead projector.

Present each dialog in turn. See "Presenting Dialogs" on page vii.

2. Help students read the directions. Demonstrate by circling the first item on the board or overhead projector. Then have students complete the exercise with a partner. Correct

the activity on the board or overhead projector.

3. Present or review the letter **f.** See "Presenting Letters" on page vii. Then have students complete the activity. For extra review or reinforcement, use pages 2 and 10 of the Introductory Unit.

4. Help students read the directions. Demonstrate by circling the first item on the board or overhead projector. Then have students complete the exercise independently. Ask students to correct each other's work in pairs. Write the sentence on the board or overhead projector and have a volunteer circle the answers.

5. Help students read the directions. Demonstrate by completing the first item on the board or overhead pro-

4.Circle accident **and** fire.

5.Write f. **Say the word.**

_f_ ire　　___ire　　___ire　　___ire

6.Work with a partner. Write the telephone numbers.

About You

IMPORTANT ☎ NUMBERS	
Police	
Fire Department	
Ambulance	

jector. Then have students complete the exercise independently. Check students' work. Then ask volunteers to read the word aloud and match it to a picture card.

About You **6.** Help students read the directions. Demonstrate by completing the first item on the board. Then have students complete the activity in pairs. Ask volunteers to read the answers aloud.

FOLLOW-UP

Asking for Help: Using pantomime, demonstrate making an emergency telephone call. Give the school's address as the location of the emergency. Then have pairs of students role-play making emergency telephone calls. Have them pantomime

dialing 911 on Blackline Master 2: Telephone. Have them pretend the emergency is at or near their homes and to supply this information during the telephone call. Circulate to offer help as needed.

♦ Conduct the role-plays again. This time, have students sit back-to-back so they have to talk to each other without benefit of gestures or facial cues. Have volunteers present their conversations to the class.

Work with a partner.
Make a list of telephone numbers.

	NUMBER
Police	
Ambulance	
Fire Department	
School	
Post Office	
Bank	

34

PRESENTATION

On the board or overhead projector, write the words **bank, school, post office, police,** and **ambulance.** Ask volunteers to read the words aloud and find the matching picture card for each. Help students read the directions. Demonstrate by completing the first item on the board or overhead projector.

Put students in pairs and have them help each other complete the page from the address book. Supply any numbers students need to complete the page.

Copy the page on the board or overhead projector and ask volunteers each to fill in one of the numbers. Correct them if necessary. Read the numbers aloud and have students check their own or each other's work by referring to the board or overhead projector. Then check students' lists yourself.

FOLLOW-UP

What's that Number? Ask, *What are some important telephone numbers for you?* Students might mention a day care center, a work number, a friend or relative's number, or the number of a health clinic. Write the numbers that are of general interest on the board or overhead projector under the heading **Telephone Numbers.** Give students time to copy information that might be important to them.

◆ Ask students to name other places they would like the addresses and telephone numbers of, such as a number for bus or train information. Help students find the numbers they need. Write them on the board and allow time for students to copy them.

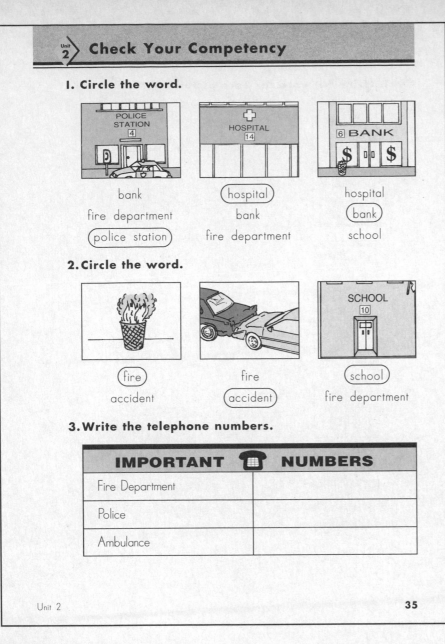

PREPARATION

Briefly review the new language in this unit before students open their books. Write the words on the board or overhead projector and ask volunteers to find the matching word cards. Then have students match word cards and picture cards.

Provide specific help as needed until you are sure students feel confident that they know all the new words.

PRESENTATION

Use any of the procedures in "Evaluation," page viii, with these pages. Record individuals' results on the Unit 2 Individual Competency Chart. Record the class's results on the Class Cumulative Competency Chart.

ENGLISH IN ACTION

An Optional Cooperative Learning Activity: Arrange students in small groups, taking care to put students who live in the same area in the same group. Ask each group to make a map of the important places in their area. Instruct them to draw in such places as the post office, bank, school, hospital, police station, fire station, and any other places that are important to them. Circulate to assist as needed. Have each group choose a member to point out key places to the class. Have students label the hospital, bank, post office, school, fire station, and police station on their maps. As an extension of this activity you might want to arrange a visit to the business district of your town.

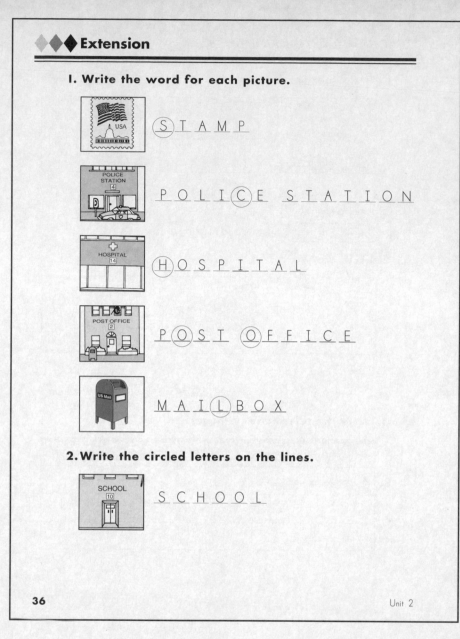

I. Write the word for each picture.

Ⓢ T A M P

P O L I Ⓒ E   S T A T I O N

Ⓗ O S P I T A L

P Ⓞ S T   Ⓞ F F I C E

M A I Ⓛ B O X

2. Write the circled letters on the lines.

S C H O O L

PREPARATION

With students, brainstorm a list of all the words they've learned in this unit. Write them on the board or overhead projector and read them aloud. Ask volunteers to find corresponding picture cards or pictures in the book.

PRESENTATION

1. Help students read the first set of directions. Demonstrate by completing the first item on the board or overhead projector. Then have students complete the activity in pairs. Have volunteers share their answers with the class.

2. Help students read the directions. Demonstrate by filling in the first letter on the board or overhead projector. Have students complete the rest of the activity in pairs. Circulate to assist as needed. Ask a volunteer to share the answers with the class.

Unit 3

School and Country

CITY ADULT SCHOOL

Look at the picture.

Where are the people?

What are they doing?

37

UNIT COMPETENCIES

1. Identify people and places at school
2. Say room numbers
3. Identify classroom objects

Unit 3 Optional Materials

● Alphabet cards for letters **i, e, c, m, r, b,** and **k.**

● Number cards for numerals **0** through **30;** corresponding picture cards showing numbers of objects from 0 to thirty.

● Picture cards and word cards for people, places, and items in a school (office, library, teacher, student, men's room, women's room, board, book, and desk) and word cards for **room** and **country.**

● Realia: classroom objects (book, eraser, notebook, paper, pen, pencil) and a large map of the world.

♦ Blackline Master 3: Classroom Objects, page 144.

Teaching Note

Use pages 8 and 9 of the Introductory Unit to clarify the direction lines in this unit.

COMPETENCIES (page 37)

Identify people and places at school

PRESENTATION

Teaching Note: Use this page to warm up students, to check and draw on their prior knowledge, and to spark interest.

Have students open their book to page 37. Read the unit title and the questions aloud. Encourage students to identify as many items in the picture as they can and to describe what is happening. As students may be able to say very little, you might have to prompt them by indicating items for them to name or by saying names of items and having students repeat them. Model any words students do

not know. Repeat students' ideas or restate them in acceptable English.

FOLLOW-UP

What's in a School? Take students for a walk around the school. Elicit names students may already know for places (such as the library or office), people (such as a teacher or a secretary), and things (such as a flag or an exit). Model any words students want to know. When you return to the classroom, ask, *What's in a school?* and write the items students name on the board or overhead projector.

♦ Have students look around the classroom and name as many objects as they can (such as a book, pencil,

or desk). Model any words students want to know. Write these words on the board or overhead projector.

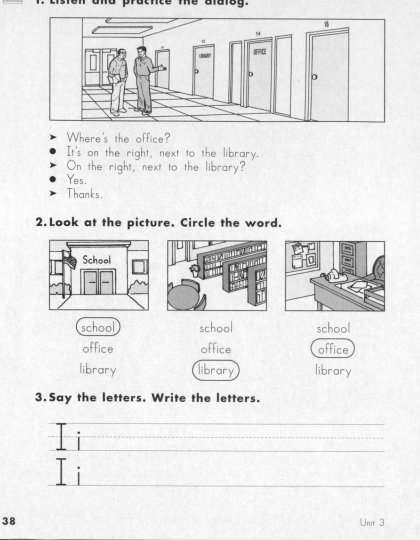

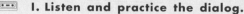

1. Listen and practice the dialog.

> ➤ Where's the office?
> ● It's on the right, next to the library.
> ➤ On the right, next to the library?
> ● Yes.
> ➤ Thanks.

2. Look at the picture. Circle the word.

(school)	school	school
office	office	(office)
library	(library)	library

3. Say the letters. Write the letters.

I i

I i

38   Unit 3

PREPARATION

Preteach the new language in the lesson. Follow these suggestions.

● Use picture cards and word cards to preteach the recognition words **office** and **library.** See "Presenting Recognition Words" on page vii.

● Preteach or review numerals **0** to **30.** Use numeral cards and/or pages 4 and 10 of the Introductory Unit.

● Preteach the dialog. Teach students the phrases **on the right** and **on the left** by using gestures and referring to classroom objects. To teach **next to,** stand beside a student and say, *I'm next to (name).* Ask volunteers to tell you who they are next to. Focus attention on the illustration and ask, *Where's the office?* Have

students repeat. Then model the answer, *It's on the right, next to the library.* Have students repeat.

PRESENTATION

1. Focus attention on the illustration. Help students identify the building and read the labels on the rooms. Have them say as much as they can about the illustration. You may want to cue students by indicating items for them to name or by saying names of items and having students indicate them. Restate students' ideas in acceptable English and write them on the board or overhead projector.

Present the dialog. See "Presenting Dialogs" on page vii.

2. Help students read the directions.

Demonstrate by completing the first item on the board or overhead projector. Then have them complete the exercise in pairs. Correct the exercise on the board or overhead projector.

3. Present or review the letter **i.** See "Presenting Letters" on page vii. Then have students complete the activity. For additional reinforcement, use pages 2 and 10 of the Introductory Unit.

4. Help students read the directions. Demonstrate by completing the first item on the board or overhead projector. Then have students complete the exercise in pairs. Correct the exercise on the board or overhead projector.

5. Help students read the directions. Demonstrate by completing the first

4. Circle OFFICE **and** LIBRARY.
Underline the room numbers.

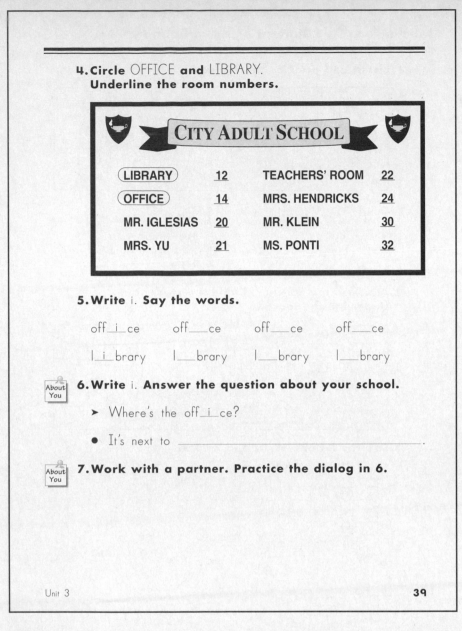

CITY ADULT SCHOOL

(LIBRARY)	12	TEACHERS' ROOM	22
(OFFICE)	14	MRS. HENDRICKS	24
MR. IGLESIAS	20	MR. KLEIN	30
MRS. YU	21	MS. PONTI	32

5. Write i. **Say the words.**

off_i_ce   off__ce   off__ce   off__ce

l_i_brary   l__brary   l__brary   l__brary

6. Write i. **Answer the question about your school.**

➤ Where's the off_i_ce?

● It's next to _____.

7. Work with a partner. Practice the dialog in 6.

item on the board or overhead projector. Then have students complete the exercise independently. Ask volunteers to read the words aloud and match them to picture cards.

6. Help students read the directions. Discuss the location of the office at your school. Draw a simple map on the board or overhead projector indicating the rooms that are adjacent to the office. Demonstrate by completing the first item on the board or overhead projector. Then have students complete the exercise in pairs. Ask volunteers to read their answers aloud.

7. Review the dialog in item 6 with the class. Then have students say the dialog in pairs, reversing roles so each student both asks

and answers the question. Circulate to offer help as needed. Ask several pairs of students to say the dialog aloud for the class.

FOLLOW-UP

At the Library: Take students to visit the school library and/or office. Model how to ask for information. In the library, show students how to check out books and magazines. When you return to the classroom, have students help you draw a diagram of the school library and/or office on the board or overhead projector.

♦ Arrange students in pairs. Have one partner play the role of a new student. The other student gives the new student information about the

library and/or office. Then have students reverse roles and repeat. Ask several pairs to repeat their conversations for the class.

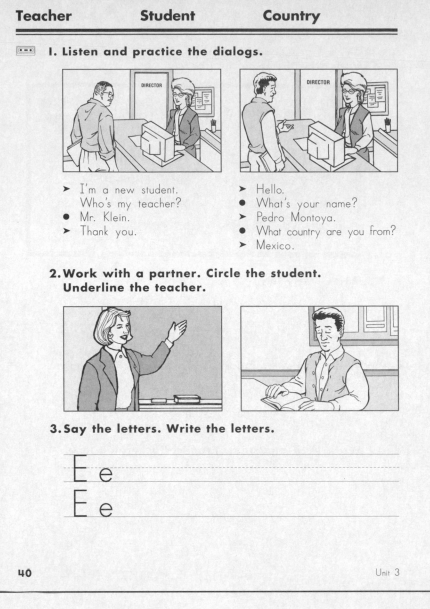

PREPARATION

Preteach the new language in the lesson. Follow these suggestions.

● Use picture cards, word cards, people in the classroom, and a map of the world to preteach the recognition words **teacher, student,** and **country.** See "Presenting Recognition Words" on page vii.

● Preteach the dialogs. To teach **who,** ask, *Who is the teacher?* Indicate yourself and answer, *I am the teacher.* Then ask, *Who is a student?* Indicate a student in the class. Teach the word **new** by holding up a copy of the Student Book, and then holding up a new book students have never seen before. Say, *This is a new book.* Say, *I'm from (the U.S.).*

Model the country each student is from. Write the names of all the countries students mention on the board or overhead projector. Then model the question, *"What country are you from?"* Have each student copy the name of his or her country. Check to make sure each student has written his or her country correctly.

PRESENTATION

1. Focus attention on the illustrations. Help students identify the room as an office in a school. Have them say as much as they can about the illustrations. You may want to cue students by indicating items for them to name or by saying names of items and having students indicate them. Restate students' ideas in

acceptable English and write them on the board or overhead projector.

Present each dialog in turn. See "Presenting Dialogs" on page vii.

2. Help students read the directions. Demonstrate the first item by sketching stick figures on the board or overhead projector and circling one of them and underlining the other. Then have students complete the exercise in pairs. Check students' work.

3. Present or review the letter **e.** See "Presenting Letters" on page vii. Then have students complete the activity. For additional review or reinforcement, use pages 2 and 10 of the Introductory Unit.

4. Help students read the directions.

4. Circle TEACHER, STUDENT, and COUNTRY.

(STUDENT): *Pedro Montoya*

(COUNTRY): *Mexico*

CITY ADULT SCHOOL
Registration Form

(TEACHER): *Mr. Klein*   LEVEL: *1*

5. Write e and c.

t_e_ach_e_r   t___ach___r   t___ach___r

stud_e_nt   stud___nt   stud___nt

_c_ountry   ___ountry   ___ountry

About You

6. Work with a partner. Complete the form.
Ask each other questions.

STUDENT : _____

COUNTRY : _____

CITY ADULT SCHOOL
Registration Form

TEACHER : _____   LEVEL: _____

About You

7. Work with a partner. Ask the questions.
Write the answers.

➤ What country are you from?

● _____

➤ Who's your teacher?

● _____

Demonstrate by circling the first item on the board or overhead projector. Then have students complete the exercise in pairs. Correct the exercise on the board or overhead projector. Then check students' work yourself.

5. Help students read the directions. Demonstrate by completing the first item on the board or overhead projector. Then have students complete the exercise independently. Check students' work.

About You **6.** Help students read the directions. Demonstrate by completing the first item on the board. Have students complete the activity. Write your name on the board or overhead projector to help students spell your name correctly. Correct students'

work. Have volunteers read their answers aloud.

About You **7.** Help students read the directions. Model asking a volunteer questions and writing the answers on the board or overhead projector. Then have students complete the exercise in pairs. Have several pairs ask and answer the questions aloud.

FOLLOW-UP

My Country: Have students bring in photographs taken in their countries of origin, items of clothing typical of their countries, or objects from their countries. Have each student in turn name his or her country, indicate it on the world map, and show what he or she brought in.

♦ Arrange students in pairs to tell

each other their countries of origin and show each other the items they've brought in. Then have pairs join to form groups of four. Within the groups, have each student tell the others what country his or her partner is from and what item his or her partner brought in.

Identify people and places at school

Say room numbers

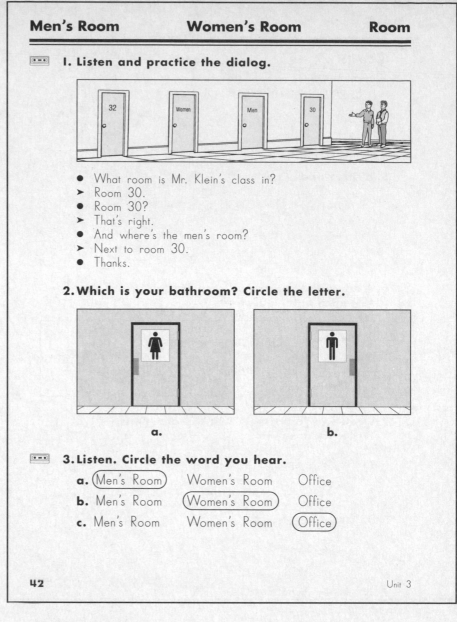

Men's Room　　　**Women's Room**　　　**Room**

[▭▭] **I. Listen and practice the dialog.**

- What room is Mr. Klein's class in?
- ➤ Room 30.
- Room 30?
- ➤ That's right.
- And where's the men's room?
- ➤ Next to room 30.
- Thanks.

2. Which is your bathroom? Circle the letter.

a.　　　　　　　　b.

[▭▭] **3. Listen. Circle the word you hear.**

a. (Men's Room)　　Women's Room　　Office

b. Men's Room　　(Women's Room)　　Office

c. Men's Room　　Women's Room　　(Office)

42　　　　　　　　　　　　　　　　　　　Unit 3

PREPARATION

Preteach the new language in the lesson. Follow these suggestions.

● Use the illustrations in this unit and refer to the room you are in to preteach the word **room.** Use picture cards and word cards to preteach the recognition words **Men's Room** and **Women's Room.** See "Presenting Recognition Words" on page vii.

Teaching Note: Students may hear men's and women's rooms called by different names. You might present a few common alternatives: **rest room, bathroom,** etc.

● Preteach the dialog. If necessary, review the phrase **next to.** See page 38. Then draw two adjacent rooms on the board. Label one with the

numeral **30** and the other with the symbol for the men's room. Ask, *Where's the men's room?* Have students repeat. Then model the answer, *Next to room 30,* and have students repeat.

PRESENTATION

1. Focus attention on the illustration. Help students read the labels on the doors. Have them say as much as they can about the illustration. Restate students' ideas in acceptable English and write them on the board or overhead projector.

Present the dialog. See "Presenting Dialogs" on page vii.

2. Help students read the directions. Demonstrate by circling the letter of

the bathroom appropriate for you on the board. Then have students complete the exercise independently. Then check students' work.

3. Help students read the directions. Then, present the listening. See "Presenting Listenings" on page vii. Correct students' work. Ask volunteers to read the correct answers aloud.

4. Present or review the letters **m** and **r.** See "Presenting Letters" on page vii. Then have students complete the activity. For additional reinforcement, use pages 2, 3 and 10 of the Introductory Unit.

[About You] **5.** Help students read the directions. Demonstrate by completing the first item on the board. Then have them complete the exercise

4. Say the letters. Write the letters.

M m ____ ____

M m

R r

R r

About You **5. Write** r. **Write the number of your room.**

My class is in __r__oom _____ .

My class is in ____oom _____ .

My class is in ____oom _____ .

About You **6. Complete the dialog.**
Ask for your bathroom.

➤ Where's the _____'s room?

● Next to _____ .

About You **7. Work with a partner. Practice the dialog in 6.**

independently. Ask volunteers to read the sentence aloud to the class.

About You **6.** Help students read the directions. Demonstrate by completing the first item on the board or overhead projector. Then have students complete the exercise independently. Ask several students to read their answers aloud.

About You **7.** Review the dialog in item 6 with the class. Then have students ask and answer the question in the dialog in pairs, reversing roles several times. Have several pairs say the dialog aloud for the class.

at various rooms to identify room numbers, teachers, and/or the purpose of the room. After you return to the classroom, have students help you draw a simple map of the school on the board or overhead projector. Mark the office, rest rooms, library, and so on. Have volunteers ask the location of these places. Have other volunteers answer.

♦ Ask students in pairs to describe the school to each other. Instruct them to say as much about it as they can. Circulate to offer help as needed. Have several volunteers describe the school aloud to the class.

FOLLOW-UP

A Tour of the School: Take your students on a tour of your school. Pause

---

Board   **Book**   **Desk**

I. Listen and practice.

➤ Please sit at this desk.

➤ Look at the board.

2. Work with a partner. What are they? Say the words.

Level 1
English

3. Say the letters. Write the letters.

B b

B b

K k

K k

44   Unit 3

PREPARATION

Preteach the new language in the lesson. Follow these suggestions.

● Use picture cards, word cards, and Blackline Master 3: Classroom Objects to preteach the recognition words **board, book,** and **desk.** See "Presenting Recognition Words" on page vii.

● Preteach the dialog by demonstrating the commands. Stand beside your desk chair. Say, *Sit at this desk* and sit down. Pantomime the other commands in the dialog. Then ask a volunteer to come forward. Repeat the commands and help the volunteer carry them out. Finally, give the whole class the commands. Repeat commands in various orders until students follow them easily.

PRESENTATION

1. Focus attention on the illustrations. Help students identify students and teachers. Have them say as much as they can about the illustrations. You may want to cue students by indicating items for them to name or by saying names of items and having students indicate them. Restate students' ideas in acceptable English and write them on the board or overhead projector.

Present the dialog. See "Presenting Dialogs" on page vii.

Teaching Note: You may want to present other common classroom language, such as: **Pass in your papers, Get out (a pencil),** and **Close your books.**

2. Help students read the directions. Demonstrate by indicating the first picture and saying the word **board.** Then have students complete the exercise in pairs. Have volunteers say the words aloud to the class.

3. Present or review the letters **b** and **k.** See "Presenting Letters" on page vii. Then have students complete the activity. For additional reinforcement, use pages 2 and 10 of the Introductory Unit.

4. Help students read the directions. Demonstrate by completing the first item on the board or overhead projector. Then have students complete the exercise independently. Check students' work. Then ask volunteers to read the words aloud and match them to picture cards.

4. **Write** b **and** k.

b oard   ___oard   ___oard   ___oard

des k   des___   des___   des___

b oo k   ___oo___   ___oo___   ___oo___

5. **Listen. Circle the number.**

a.

GOOD Morning

1.   ②

b.

My name is Pedro

①   2.

6. **Work with a partner.**
Circle the board, book, and desk.
Underline the student and teacher.

Unit 3   **45**

---

5. Help students read the directions. Then, present the listening. See "Presenting Listenings" on page vii. Correct students' work. Ask volunteers to read the correct answers aloud.

6. Focus attention on the illustration. Have students describe it in as much detail as they can. Then help them read the directions. Demonstrate by circling the first item on the board or overhead projector. Have students complete the activity in pairs. Correct the activity on the board or overhead projector. Check students' work.

For example, say, *Pick up your book.* First, give the command and demonstrate the action yourself. Then ask the class to perform the action with you. Finally, give the command without visual cues and have students carry it out.

♦ Have students in pairs take turns giving each other commands. Then have students change partners and repeat the activity. Circulate to assist as needed. Ask several pairs to demonstrate the activity to the class.

FOLLOW-UP

Following Instructions: Give a series of commands for students to follow.

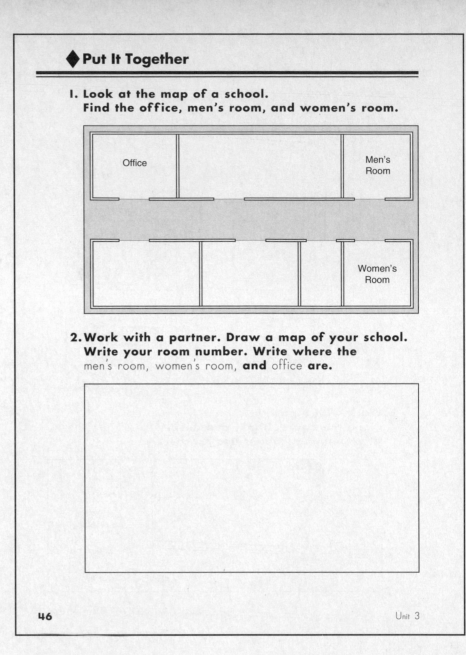

◆ Put It Together

**I. Look at the map of a school.
Find the office, men's room, and women's room.**

Office				Men's Room

				Women's Room

**2. Work with a partner. Draw a map of your school.
Write your room number. Write where the**
men's room, women's room, **and** office **are.**

PREPARATION

On the board or overhead projector, write the words **men's room, women's room,** and **office.** Ask volunteers to read the words aloud and to find the matching picture cards.

If you did not do the Follow-Up activity on page 44 with your students, you may wish to take them on a tour of the school before they begin this activity.

PRESENTATION

1. Help students read the directions. Focus attention on the floor plan of the school. Ask students to say as much as they can about it. Restate students' ideas in acceptable English and write them on the board or overhead projector.

2. Arrange students in pairs to draw maps of your school. Circulate to assist as needed. Ask several volunteers to draw their maps on the board or overhead projector and describe them to the class.

FOLLOW-UP

A New Student at School: Accompany students to the outside entrance of your school. Play the role of a new student coming to your school for the first time. Ask the location of some place in the school and have a volunteer provide an answer. Repeat several times, asking different questions each time. Then have students enact the scene in pairs. Circulate to offer help as needed. Have students switch roles and repeat the activity.

◆ In the classroom, arrange students in small groups. Instruct them to designate one student as the new student. Have the other group members tell the new student as much as they can about the school. Ask groups to repeat their conversations for the class.

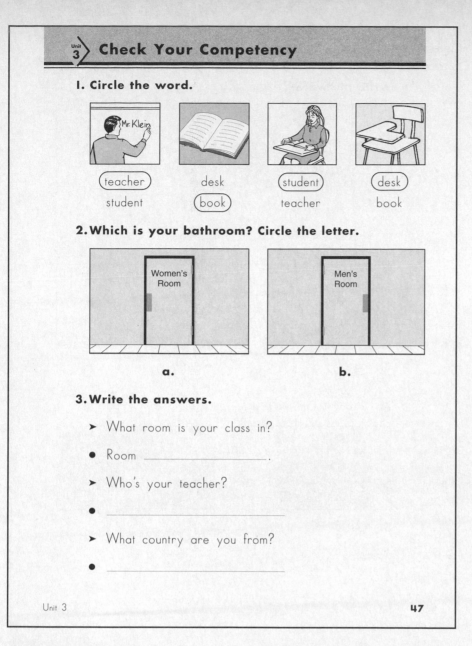

1. Circle the word.

(teacher)   desk   (student)   (desk)
student   (book)   teacher   book

2. Which is your bathroom? Circle the letter.

Women's Room

Men's Room

a.   b.

3. Write the answers.

➤ What room is your class in?

● Room _____.

➤ Who's your teacher?

● _____

➤ What country are you from?

● _____

Unit 3   **47**

PREPARATION

Briefly review the new language in this unit before students open their books. Write the words on the board or overhead projector and ask volunteers to find the matching word cards and picture cards or to indicate appropriate people or objects in the classroom. Review the number of your classroom and the spelling of your name. Make sure each student can write the name of the country he or she is from.

Provide specific help as needed until you are sure students feel confident that they know all the new language.

PRESENTATION

Use any of the procedures in "Evaluation," page viii, with these pages. Record individuals' results on the Unit 3 Individual Competency Chart. Record the class's results on the Class Cumulative Competency Chart.

ENGLISH IN ACTION

An Optional Cooperative Learning Activity: Walk with students around the outside of your school. Note the entrances, exits, streets, and parking lot. Return to the class and arrange students in small groups. Have them make maps of the outside of your school. Circulate to assist as needed. Ask a member of each group to draw the group's map on the board or overhead projector. Ask another member of each group to describe the group's map to the class.

Write the words.

1. fficoe

o_f_ _f_i_c_e

2. skde

de_s_ _k

3. kobo

b_ _oo_ k

4. eatchre

tea_c_h_e_r

5. tsdentu

_s_tude_ _n_ t

6. lbriary

l_i_ _br_ a_ ry

PREPARATION

With students, brainstorm a list of all the words they've learned in this unit. Write them on the board or overhead projector and read them aloud. Ask volunteers to find corresponding picture cards or pictures in the book or to gesture toward appropriate objects or people.

PRESENTATION

Help students read the directions. Demonstrate by completing the first item on the board. Have students complete the activity in pairs. Circulate to assist as needed. Ask volunteers to read their answers aloud to the class.

Daily Living

Look at the picture.

Where are the people?

What are they doing?

49

Unit 4 Overview

UNIT COMPETENCIES

1. Ask for, say, and write the time
2. Ask for, say, and write the day of the week
3. Ask for, say, and write the date

Unit 4 Optional Materials

● Alphabet cards for letters **d, w, y, j, u,** and **v.**

● Number cards for numerals **0** to **30** and **40, 50, 60, 70, 80,** and **90.**

● Word cards for **time, date, today, tomorrow, date of birth, month, year** and for each day of the week and month of the year.

● Realia: Clocks and watches; a large wall calendar for the year.

◆ Blackline Master 4: Clock, page 145.

Teaching Note

Use pages 8 and 9 of the Introductory Unit as needed to clarify the direction lines in this unit to students.

COMPETENCIES (page 49)

Ask for and say the time

PRESENTATION

Teaching Note: Use this page to warm up students, to check and draw on their prior knowledge, and to spark interest.

Have students open their books to page 49. Read the unit title and the questions aloud. Encourage students to identify as many items in the picture as they can and to describe what is happening. As students may be able to say very little, you might have to prompt them by indicating items for them to name or by saying names of items and having students repeat them. Repeat students' ideas or

restate them in acceptable English.

FOLLOW-UP

How Do You Get to School? Ask students how they get to school. Have available pictures of a car, a train, a bus, a bicycle, a motorcycle, and a person walking. Have each student in turn use the pictures to indicate his or her mode of transportation. Model the names of any types of transportation students want to know.

◆ Arrange students in pairs to ask and answer questions about the way they and other members of their families get to school and/or work. Circulate to assist as needed. Ask volunteers to repeat their conversations for the class.

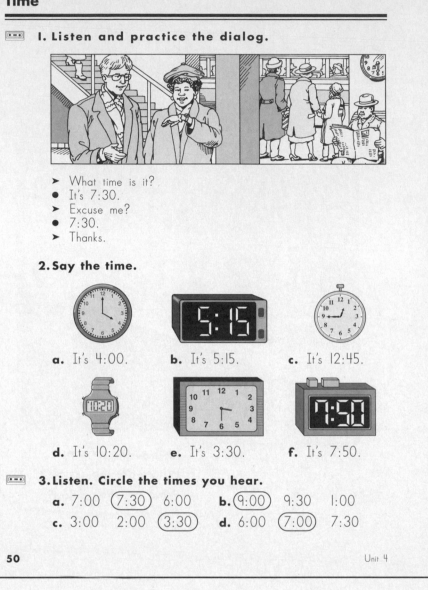

Time

⊡ I. Listen and practice the dialog.

➤ What time is it?
● It's 7:30.
➤ Excuse me?
● 7:30.
➤ Thanks.

2. Say the time.

a. It's 4:00.   **b.** It's 5:15.   **c.** It's 12:45.

d. It's 10:20.   **e.** It's 3:30.   **f.** It's 7:50.

⊡ 3. Listen. Circle the times you hear.

a. 7:00   (7:30)   6:00   **b.** (9:00)   9:30   1:00
c. 3:00   2:00   (3:30)   **d.** 6:00   (7:00)   7:30

50   Unit 4

PREPARATION

Preteach the new language in the lesson. Follow these suggestions.

● Use the word card, realia clocks and watches, Blackline Master 4: Clock, and the illustrations on the page to preteach the recognition word **time.** See "Presenting Recognition Words" on page vii.

● Preteach or review numerals **0** to **60.** For additional reinforcement, use pages 4 and 10 of the Introductory Unit.

● Use Blackline Master 4: Clock to teach students to tell time. First, set the clock to an hour. Say *It's (nine) o'clock* and have students repeat. Proceed through the hours in order, then out of order, until students

name the hour easily. Repeat the procedure for some half hours, quarter hours, and five minute intervals saying *It's (nine-o-five, nine-fifteen, nine-thirty).*

Teaching Note: You may want to teach students to tell time over several days rather than all at once.

● Preteach the dialog. Set the hands of the blackline master clock to 7:30. Point to the clock and ask, *What time is it?* Have students repeat. Model the answer, *It's 7:30.* Then cup your hand around your ear, ask, *Excuse me?* and have students repeat. Then say the time again.

PRESENTATION

1. Focus attention on the illustration.

Have students say as much as they can about it. You may want to cue students by indicating items for them to name or by saying names of items and having students indicate them. Restate students' ideas in acceptable English and write them on the board or overhead projector.

Present the dialog. See "Presenting Dialogs" on page vii.

2. Help students read the directions. Demonstrate by saying the time of the first item. Then have students complete the exercise in pairs. Have volunteers say the times aloud.

3. Help students read the directions. Then, present the listening. See "Presenting Listenings" on page vii. Correct students' work. Ask volun-

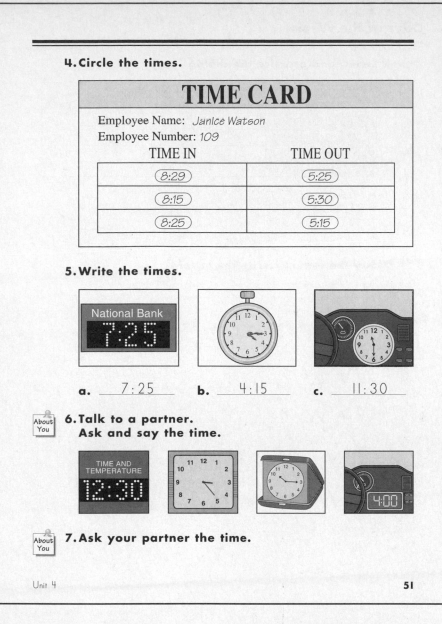

4. Circle the times.

TIME CARD

Employee Name: *Janice Watson*

Employee Number: *109*

TIME IN	TIME OUT
(8:29)	(5:25)
(8:15)	(5:30)
(8:25)	(5:15)

5. Write the times.

National Bank 7:25

a. 7:25   b. 4:15   c. 11:30

6. Talk to a partner.
Ask and say the time.

TIME AND TEMPERATURE 12:30   4:00

7. Ask your partner the time.

Unit 4   **51**

---

teers to read the correct answers aloud.

4. Help students read the directions. Demonstrate by circling the first item on the board or overhead projector. Then have students complete the exercise. Correct the exercise on the board or overhead projector and have volunteers read the times aloud.

5. Help students read the directions and identify the situations. Demonstrate by completing the first item on the board or overhead projector. Then have students complete the exercise. Write the answers on the board or overhead projector and have volunteers say the times aloud.

6. Help students read the directions. Ask a volunteer to help

you demonstrate the first item. Then have students complete the exercise. Have students change partners and repeat the exercise. Ask several pairs to repeat their conversations aloud.

7. Help students read the directions. Model by asking a student to say the time. Then have students complete the activity in pairs. Have one or two pairs repeat their conversations for the class.

FOLLOW-UP

More Clocks: Arrange students in pairs. Give each student a copy of Blackline Master 4: Clock. Have partners take turns setting the time on their clocks and asking their partners the time. Have students change partners and repeat the activity.

Circulate to assist as needed.

♦ Have students take turns setting the time on their clocks for their partners to say and write the times.

Days of the Week

🔲 **I. Listen and practice the dialog.**

Fall Class Schedule						
COMMUNITY LEARNING CENTER FALL CLASS SCHEDULE	MON.	TUES.	WED.	THURS.	FRI.	SAT.
ESL 1		10:00		10:00		
ESL 2	11:00		11:00			
ESL 3						9:00
ESL 4			1:00			

➤ When is your English class?
● My class is on Monday and Wednesday.
  How about you?
➤ My class is on Tuesday and Thursday.

2. Say the letters. Write the letters.

D d

D d

W w

W w

Y y

Y y

PREPARATION

Preteach the new language in the lesson. Follow these suggestions.

● Focus attention on the calendar you brought in. Indicate each day of the week in order. Model the day and have students repeat. Continue until students can say the days of the week in order easily. Then hold up word cards for the days of the week in and out of order. Ask, *What day is it?* Continue until students can read the days of the week easily.

● Provide pairs of students with flash cards for the days of the week. Ask partners to take turns holding up cards and asking and answering the question, *What day is it?* Circulate to assist as needed.

● Preteach the dialog. To teach the phrase **How about you?** choose one student and ask, *When is your English class?* Help the student answer. Then indicate another student and ask, *How about you?* Help the student answer.

PRESENTATION

1. Focus attention on the illustration. Help students identify the situation. Have them say as much as they can about the illustration. You may want to cue students by indicating items for them to name or by saying names of items and having students indicate them. Restate students' ideas in acceptable English and write them on the board or overhead projector.

Present the dialog. See "Presenting Dialogs" on page vii.

2. Present or review the letters **d, w,** and **y.** See "Presenting Letters" on page vii. Then have students complete the activity. For additional reinforcement, use pages 2, 3, and 10 of the Introductory Unit.

3. Help students read the directions. Demonstrate by completing the first item on the board or overhead projector. Then have students complete the exercise independently. Check students' work. Ask volunteers to read the words aloud and indicate the days on the calendar.

4. Help students read the directions. Demonstrate by completing the item on the board or overhead projector. Then have students complete the

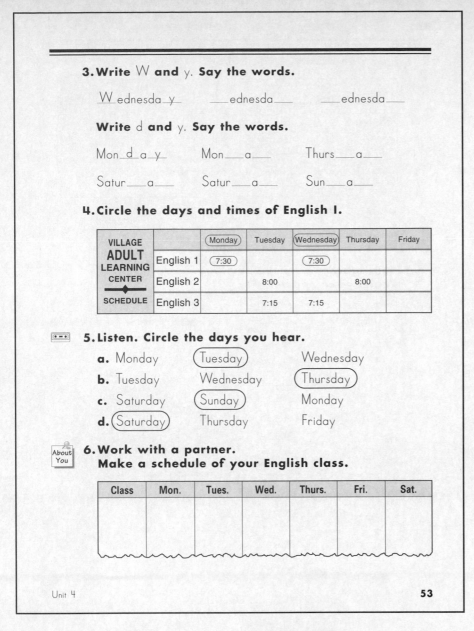

3. Write W and y. **Say the words.**

W_ednesda_y   ___ednesda___   ___ednesda___

Write d **and** y. **Say the words.**

Mon_d_a_y   Mon___a___   Thurs___a___

Satur___a___   Satur___a___   Sun___a___

4. Circle the days and times of English 1.

VILLAGE **ADULT** LEARNING CENTER ◆ SCHEDULE		(Monday)	Tuesday	(Wednesday)	Thursday	Friday
	English 1	(7:30)		(7:30)		
	English 2		8:00		8:00	
	English 3		7:15	7:15		

5. Listen. Circle the days you hear.

a. Monday   (Tuesday)   Wednesday

b. Tuesday   Wednesday   (Thursday)

c. Saturday   (Sunday)   Monday

d. (Saturday)   Thursday   Friday

6. Work with a partner.
Make a schedule of your English class.

Class	Mon.	Tues.	Wed.	Thurs.	Fri.	Sat.

exercise. Check students' work. Have volunteers read the answers aloud.

5. Help students read the directions. Then, present the listening. See "Presenting Listenings" on page vii. Correct students' work. Ask volunteers to read their answers aloud.

6. Help students read the directions. Copy the schedule form on the board or overhead projector. Demonstrate by filling in the first time your class meets. Then have students complete the exercise. Ask a volunteer to come forward to complete the schedule on the board or overhead projector. Read the answers aloud.

FOLLOW-UP

Ordering the Days of the Week:
Have seven students come forward. Give each student a different word card with a day of the week. Have students arrange themselves in order by day of the week. Have the rest of the class verify that the students are in the correct order.

♦ Give each pair of students a set of flash cards with the days of the week written on them (make flash cards on 3" by 5" cards). Have students shuffle the cards and reorder them correctly beginning with **Sunday.** Have students change partners and repeat the activity several times.

Date   Today   Tomorrow

🔲 **I. Listen and practice the dialog.**

			May			
S	M	T	W	T	F	S
	1	2	3	4	5	6
7	8	9	10	11	12	13
14	15	16	17	18	19	20
21	22	23	24	25	26	27
28	29	30	31			

➤ What's today's date?
● May 14.
➤ Oh, no. Tomorrow is my sister's birthday.

**2. Your teacher says the numbers.
You say the numbers.**

1st	20th	30th
2nd	21st	31st
3rd	22nd	
4th	23rd	
	24th	

🔲 **3. Listen. Circle the date you hear.**

a. July 1   July 2   (July 3)   July 4
b. (June 9)   June 10   June 11   June 12
c. October 11   (October 12)   October 13   October 15
d. July 5   (July 15)   July 17   July 19

54   Unit 4

PREPARATION

Preteach the new language in the lesson. Follow these suggestions.

● Teach the word **today** by saying *Today is (Thursday).* Hold up the word card for **today.** Model the word and have students repeat. Similarly, teach the word **tomorrow.** Then teach **date.** Indicate the appropriate day on the calendar and say, *Today's date is (date).* Indicate the next day and say, *Tomorrow's date is (date).* Hold up the word card for **date.** Say the word and have students repeat.

● Preteach the ordinal numbers. Ask, *What's today's date?* Model the answer, *Today is (date),* and have students repeat. Point to each day of the current month on the calendar.

Model each date and have students repeat.

● To teach the names of the months, focus attention on the calendar. Indicate and say each month in order. Have students repeat. Then, hold up word cards for the months, in and out of order, and have students say the months. Continue until students can read the months easily.

Teaching Note: You may wish to teach the ordinal numbers and months over the course of several days rather than all at once.

● Preteach the dialog. To teach **sister,** show a photograph of your or another family. (Or draw stick figures of a family on the board or overhead projector.) Indicate one of the people and say, *This is (name).*

Then indicate a sister and say, *This is (name's) sister.* To teach **birthday,** tell students your own (or a fictitious) age. Then find your birthday on the calendar. Indicate the date and say, *This is my birthday. I will be (age at birthday).*

Pantomime dropping something. Then present **Oh, no!** by throwing up your hands and affecting a pained expression as you say the phrase. Have students repeat. Finally, say, *Oh, no! Tomorrow's my sister's birthday.* Have students repeat.

PRESENTATION

1. Focus attention on the illustrations. Have them say as much as they can about the illustrations. You may want to cue students by indicating

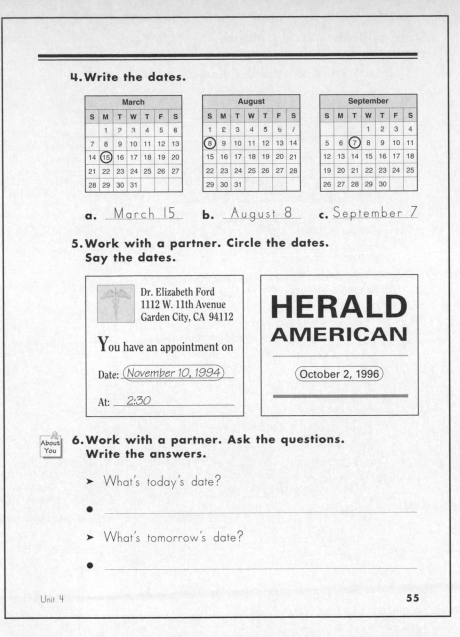

4. Write the dates.

		March				
S	M	T	W	T	F	S
	1	2	3	4	5	6
7	8	9	10	11	12	13
14	(15)	16	17	18	19	20
21	22	23	24	25	26	27
28	29	30	31			

		August				
S	M	T	W	T	F	S
1	2	3	4	5	6	7
(8)	9	10	11	12	13	14
15	16	17	18	19	20	21
22	23	24	25	26	27	28
29	30	31				

		September				
S	M	T	W	T	F	S
			1	2	3	4
5	6	(7)	8	9	10	11
12	13	14	15	16	17	18
19	20	21	22	23	24	25
26	27	28	29	30		

a. March 15 **b.** August 8 **c.** September 7

5. Work with a partner. Circle the dates. Say the dates.

Dr. Elizabeth Ford
1112 W. 11th Avenue
Garden City, CA 94112

You have an appointment on

Date: (November 10, 1994)

At: 2:30

HERALD AMERICAN

(October 2, 1996)

6. Work with a partner. Ask the questions. Write the answers.

➤ What's today's date?

● _____

➤ What's tomorrow's date?

● _____

---

items for them to name or by saying names of items and having students indicate them. Restate students' ideas in acceptable English and write them on the board or overhead projector.

Present the dialog. See "Presenting Dialogs" on page vii.

2. Help students read the directions. Say each number and have students repeat.

3. Help students read the directions. Then, present the listening. See "Presenting Listenings" on page vii. Correct students' work. Ask volunteers to read the correct answers aloud.

4. Help students read the directions. Demonstrate by completing the first item on the board or overhead pro-jector. Then have students complete the exercise. Correct on the board or overhead projector. Ask volunteers to read their answers aloud.

5. Help students read the directions. Demonstrate by circling the first item on the board or overhead pro-jector. Then have students complete the exercise. Correct the exercise on the board or overhead projector and have several pairs say their conversa-tions for the class.

6. Help students read the direc-tions. Demonstrate asking and answering the first question with a volunteer. Write the answer on the board or overhead projector. Then have students complete the exercise. Ask pairs of students to say their conversations for the class.

FOLLOW-UP

Your Birthday: Have students say their birthdays. Make a list of the dates on the board or overhead projector. Read the dates aloud and have students repeat. Discuss birthday celebrations. Encourage students to say as much as they can about birthday celebrations in their countries.

◆ Have students talk to each other to find out each other's birthdays. Ask them to line up in the order in which their birthdays will occur. Check the order by having each stu-dent in the line say his or her birth-day aloud.

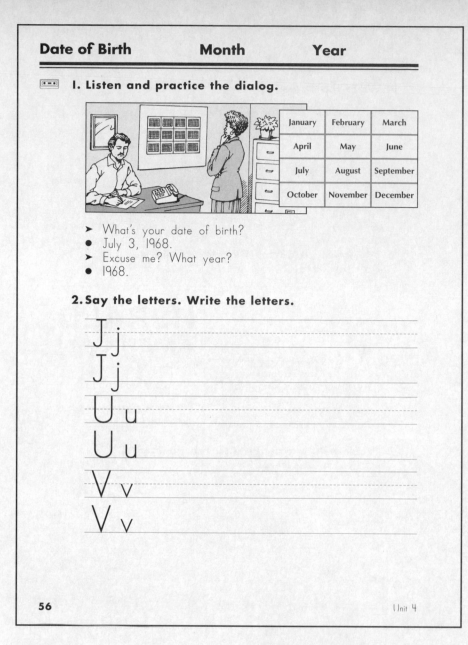

Date of Birth   Month   Year

🔊 **I. Listen and practice the dialog.**

January	February	March
April	May	June
July	August	September
October	November	December

➤ What's your date of birth?
● July 3, 1968.
➤ Excuse me? What year?
● 1968.

2. Say the letters. Write the letters.

J j

J j

U u

U u

V v

V v

56   Unit 4

PREPARATION

Preteach the new language in the lesson. Follow these suggestions.

● To teach **month** and **year,** write a few dates on the board or overhead projector. Say, *This is the month,* as you indicate the month in each date. Repeat for the year. Write additional dates on the board and ask volunteers to come forward, one at a time, and indicate the month and year in each date.

● To teach **date of birth**, say, *My birthday is (month and day).* Write the date on the board or overhead projector and read it aloud. Then say, *My date of birth is (month, day, and actual or fictitious year).* Write the date on the board or overhead

projector and read it aloud.

Teaching Note: You and your students should feel free to use fictitious information when giving ages or dates of birth.

● Preteach or review numerals **0** to **99.** For additional reinforcement, use pages 4 and 10 of the Introductory Unit.

● Preteach the dialog. Explain that a year is usually pronounced in two parts, with the first two numbers read together as one number and the second two read together as another number. Write **1968** on the board and model the pronunciation. Have students repeat. Continue writing years and having students say them until they can read years easily.

PRESENTATION

1. Focus attention on the illustrations. Have students say as much as they can about the illustrations. You may want to cue students by indicating items for them to name or by saying names of items and having students indicate them. Restate students' ideas in acceptable English and write them on the board or overhead projector.

Present the dialog. See "Presenting Dialogs" on page vii.

2. Present or review the letters **j, u,** and **v.** See "Presenting Letters" on page vii. Then have students complete the activity. For additional reinforcement, use pages 2, 3, and 10 of the Introductory Unit.

3. Write J and u. Say the words.

J u ne   ___ ___ ne   ___ ___ ne   ___ ___ ne

J u ly   ___ ___ ly   ___ ___ ly   ___ ___ ly

Write v. Say the word.

No v ember   No ___ ember   No ___ ember

No ___ ember   No ___ ember   No ___ ember

4. Look at Ellen's date of birth.

Date of birth: _____ March 17, 1966 _____

Write your date of birth: _____

5. Talk to other students. Complete the chart.

About You

BIRTHDAYS

Name	Month	Day
Maria	March	2

3. Help students read the directions. Demonstrate by completing the first item on the board or overhead projector. Then have students complete the exercise. Check students' work by copying the lists on the board or overhead projector and having students come forward, one at a time, to complete the items.

4. Help students read the directions. Demonstrate by completing the item on the board or overhead projector. Then have students complete the exercise. Check students' work. Then have volunteers read their dates of birth to the class.

About You **5.** Help students read the directions. Model talking to a volunteer to find out his or her birthday. Then demonstrate writing his or her name and birthday on the board or overhead projector. Have students complete the activity. Circulate to assist as needed. Then draw the chart on the board or overhead projector and have each student fill in his or her name and birthday. Have students use the chart on the board or overhead projector to check their work. Then check students' work yourself.

FOLLOW-UP

How Many Birthdays? Use the name of each month as the heading of a column on the board or overhead projector. Ask students to write their names under the month of their birth. Have volunteers count and tell you how many students were born in each month. Write the number on the board next to each heading.

♦ Help the class sequence the list of birthdays by month and day.

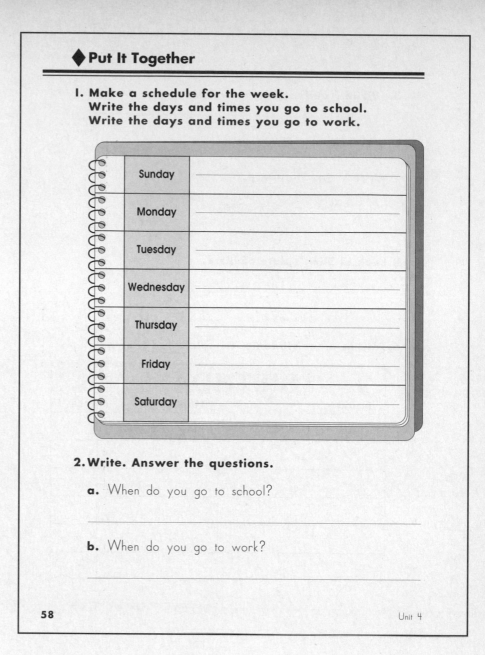

◆ **Put It Together**

I. Make a schedule for the week.
Write the days and times you go to school.
Write the days and times you go to work.

Sunday	
Monday	
Tuesday	
Wednesday	
Thursday	
Friday	
Saturday	

2. Write. Answer the questions.

a. When do you go to school?

_____

b. When do you go to work?

_____

Unit 4

PREPARATION

Refer to the wall calendar. Ask, *What day is it today? Tomorrow? What day was it yesterday? What days do we have class? What days do you go to work?* Encourage a variety of responses.

PRESENTATION

1. Help students read the directions. Demonstrate on the board or overhead projector using personal or made-up information as an example.

Have students complete the activity. Check students' work.

2. Help students read the directions. Demonstrate by completing the items on the board or overhead projector. Then have students complete

the items independently. Check students' work. Have volunteers read their answers aloud.

FOLLOW-UP

Interviews: Arrange students in pairs to interview each other about their schedules. Have them ask each other, for each day of the week, *What do you do on (Monday)?* Have students change partners and repeat the activity. Have volunteers say their conversations for the class.

◆ Have each student tell the class as a whole what his or her partner does on a certain day.

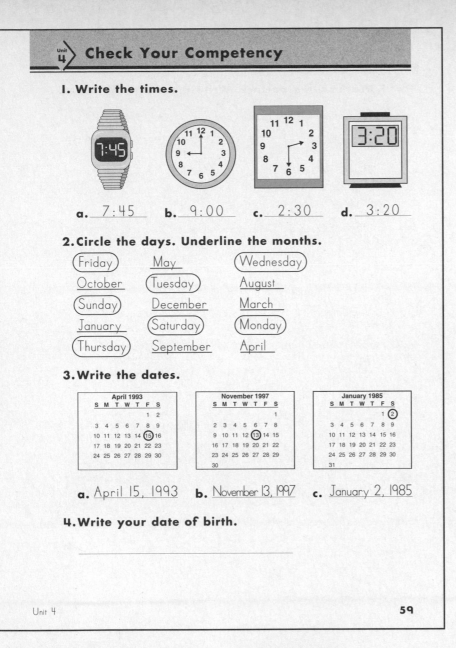

PREPARATION

Use Blackline Master 4: Clock. Set the clock to different times. Have students say the times aloud and write them on the board or overhead projector.

Use a calendar to review the days of the week and the months of the year. Point out several dates on the calendar. Ask volunteers to write them on the board or overhead projector.

Ask volunteers to write their dates of birth on the board or overhead projector. Read the dates aloud with the class.

Provide specific help as needed until you are sure students feel confident that they know how to say and write dates and times.

PRESENTATION

Use any of the procedures in "Evaluation," page viii, with these pages. Record individuals' results on the Unit 4 Individual Competency Chart. Record the class's results on the Class Cumulative Competency Chart.

ENGLISH IN ACTION

An Optional Cooperative Learning Activity: Make copies of the schedule on page 58 of this unit. With the class, brainstorm a list of activities during a day, such as **breakfast, school, lunch, work, dinner, television,** and **sleep**. Model any words students want to know. Write the words on the board or overhead projector. Arrange students in small groups and give each group a copy of the schedule. Have each group plan a typical day and enter the activities on the schedule. Circulate to assist as needed. When the groups have completed their schedules, ask each group to choose a student to read the schedule aloud.

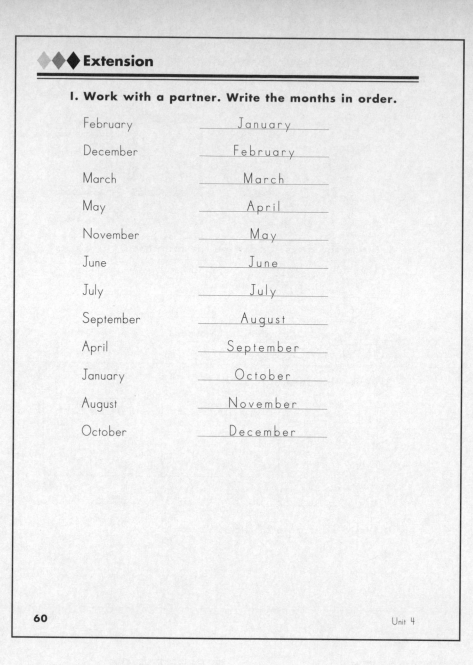

1. Work with a partner. Write the months in order.

February	January
December	February
March	March
May	April
November	May
June	June
July	July
September	August
April	September
January	October
August	November
October	December

60   Unit 4

PREPARATION

With students, brainstorm the words
they learned in this unit. Write them
on the board or overhead projector.
Have students illustrate the meaning
of the words by referring to the
blackline master clock, the wall calendar, and/or pictures in the book.

PRESENTATION

Help students read the directions.
Demonstrate by completing the first
item on the board. Have students
complete the activity in pairs.
Circulate to assist as needed. Have
volunteers read their answers to the
class. Then check students' work
yourself.

Look at the picture.

Where are the people?

What are they doing?

61

Unit 5 Overview

UNIT COMPETENCIES

1. Identify kinds of food
2. Identify kinds of food packaging
3. Ask where things are in a store
4. Comparison shop

Unit 5 Optional Materials

● Number cards for numerals **1** through **99.**

● Alphabet cards for letters **g, x, q,** and **z.**

● Picture cards (and/or realia) and word cards for food (apples, bananas, oranges, onions, tomatoes, potatoes, milk, eggs, chicken, ground beef, rice, bread, cereal, juice) and food containers (box, bag, bottle).

● Word cards for supermarket sections **(Meat, Dairy, Fruit and Vegetables),** the symbols **$** and **¢, aisle, supermarket,** and **sale.**

● Realia: Newspaper ads and/or flyers for sales at supermarkets; a box of muffin mix; a variety of bills and coins.

◆ Blackline Master 5: Money, page 146.

COMPETENCIES (page 61)

Identify kinds of food

PRESENTATION

Teaching Note: Use this page to warm up students, to check and draw on their prior knowledge, and to spark interest.

Read the unit title and questions aloud. Encourage students to identify as many items in the picture as they can and to describe what is happening. As students may be able to say very little, you might have to prompt them by indicating items for them to name or by saying names of items and having students indicate them. Ask students what food they want. Model any words students do not know. Repeat students' ideas or restate them in acceptable English.

FOLLOW-UP

What Do You Like to Eat? Arrange students in pairs. Have them take turns indicating food in the illustration on this page, naming the food item, and saying if the food is one they like. Circulate to assist as needed. Have students change partners and repeat the activity. Then ask volunteers to tell the class the food they like to eat.

◆ Bring in a variety of real food or pictures of food. Have students name as many as they can. Model any words students want to know.

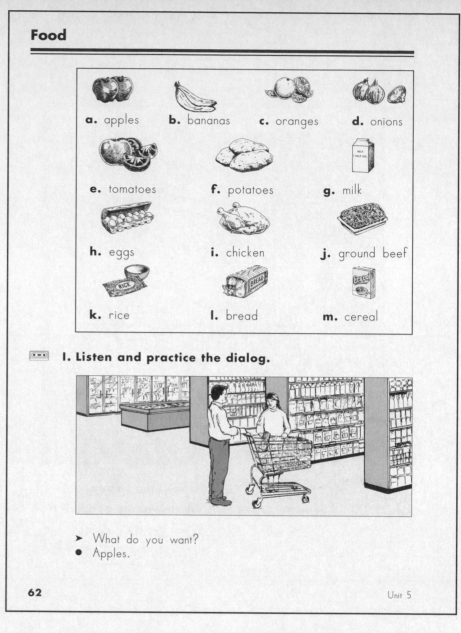

Food

a. apples b. bananas c. oranges d. onions

e. tomatoes f. potatoes g. milk

h. eggs i. chicken j. ground beef

k. rice l. bread m. cereal

1. Listen and practice the dialog.

➤ What do you want?
● Apples.

62   Unit 5

PREPARATION

Preteach the new language in the lesson. Follow these suggestions.

● Use picture cards and word cards to preteach the recognition words **apples, bananas, oranges, onions, tomatoes, potatoes, milk, eggs, chicken, ground beef, rice, bread,** and **cereal.** See "Presenting Recognition Words" on page vii.

● Preteach the dialog. To teach the word **want,** place several food items or pictures of food on display. Indicate each in turn and ask, *Do I want (item)?* Answer *No* to the first several items and leave them where they are. Then answer, *Yes, I want (item),* and take it from the display. Replace the food or pictures and ask a volunteer, *What do you want?* Help the

volunteer choose an item and name it. Repeat with different students.

PRESENTATION

1. Focus attention on the illustration. Help students read the labels aloud. Say the labels and have students identify the appropriate pictures by letter. Then say the letters and have students name the food.

Present the dialog. See "Presenting Dialogs" on page vii.

2. Help students read the directions. Demonstrate by completing the first item on the board or overhead projector. Then have students complete the exercise. Ask volunteers to read their answers to the class.

3. Help students read the directions.

Then present the listening. See "Presenting Listenings" on page vii. Check students' work. Ask volunteers to read the correct answers aloud.

4. Help students read the directions. Then model by writing the exercise on the board and saying *I want chicken.* Then write 4 in the first box. Have students complete the exercise. Check students' work.

FOLLOW-UP

What Do You Want? Arrange students in small groups. Provide each group with pictures of food and/or real food. Have each student in the group, in turn, hold up three items and ask the student next to him or

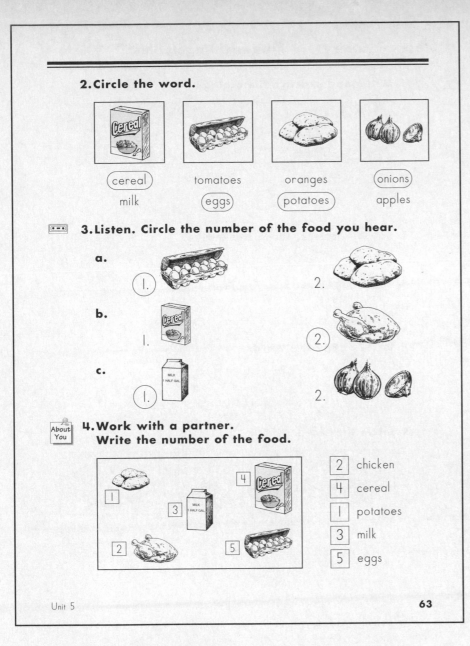

2. Circle the word.

(cereal)   tomatoes   oranges   (onions)
milk   (eggs)   (potatoes) apples

3. Listen. Circle the number of the food you hear.

a.   (1.)   2.

b.   1.   (2.)

c.   (1.)   2.

About You

4. Work with a partner.
Write the number of the food.

2 chicken
4 cereal
1 potatoes
3 milk
5 eggs

Unit 5   **63**

her, *What do you want?* The student answers by indicating an item and naming it. Circulate to assist as needed. Finally, have each student hold up the item he or she wanted and name it for the class.

♦ Have each group write a list of the food items its members wanted. Ask each group to choose a volunteer to write the list on the board or overhead projector and read it aloud.

Identify kinds of food

Ask where things are in a store

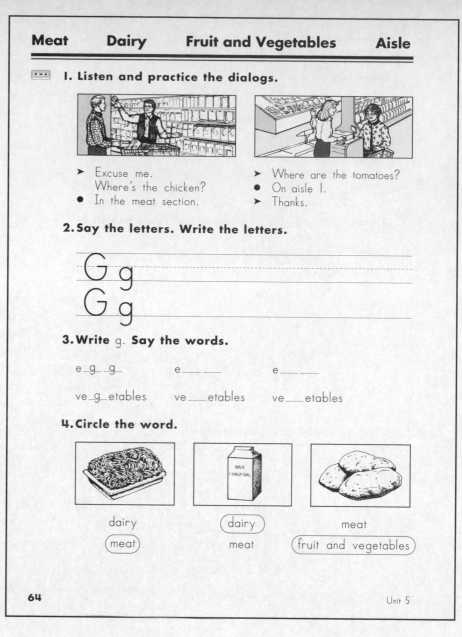

Meat   Dairy   Fruit and Vegetables   Aisle

I. Listen and practice the dialogs.

➤ Excuse me.
  Where's the chicken?
● In the meat section.

➤ Where are the tomatoes?
● On aisle I.
➤ Thanks.

2. Say the letters. Write the letters.

G g
G g

3. Write g. **Say the words.**

e_g_g   e____   e____

ve_g_etables   ve__etables   ve__etables

4. Circle the word.

dairy
(meat)

(dairy)
meat

meat
(fruit and vegetables)

64   Unit 5

PREPARATION

Preteach the new language in the lesson. Follow these suggestions.

● Use picture cards, real food, word cards, and the illustration on this page to preteach the recognition words **meat, dairy, fruit and vegetables,** and **aisle.** See "Presenting Recognition Words" on page vii.

● Preteach the dialogs. Use a picture of a supermarket or the illustration on this page to preteach the word **section.** Read the signs and aisle numbers for each section. Then ask a volunteer to come forward and face away from you. Tap the volunteer on the shoulder and say, *Excuse me. Where's the chicken?* Have students repeat. Then model the answer, *In the meat section.* Have students

repeat. Continue similarly with tomatoes.

PRESENTATION

1. Focus attention on the illustrations. Help students identify the food items and their locations. Have them say as much as they can about the illustrations. You may want to cue students by indicating items for them to name or by saying names of items and having students indicate them. Restate students' ideas in acceptable English and write them on the board or overhead projector.

Present each dialog in turn. See "Presenting Dialogs" on page vii.

2. Present or review the letter **g.** See "Presenting Letters" on page vii.

Then have students complete the activity. For additional reinforcement, use pages 2 and 10 of the Introductory Unit.

3. Help students read the directions. Demonstrate by completing the first item on the board or overhead projector. Then have them complete the exercise independently. Check students' work. Then ask volunteers to read the words aloud and match them to picture cards or illustrations in their books.

4. Help students read the directions. Demonstrate by completing the first item on the board or overhead projector. Then have students complete the exercise independently. Ask volunteers to say the words aloud.

5. Help students read the directions.

5. Circle Meat, Fruit, **and** Dairy.

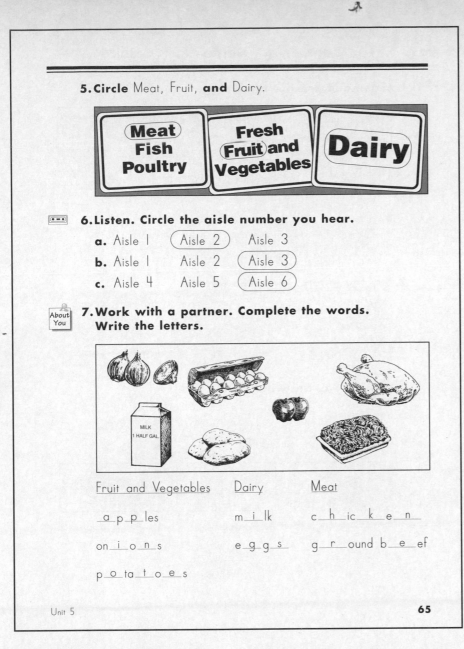

6. Listen. Circle the aisle number you hear.

a. Aisle 1   (Aisle 2)   Aisle 3

b. Aisle 1   Aisle 2   (Aisle 3)

c. Aisle 4   Aisle 5   (Aisle 6)

About You **7. Work with a partner. Complete the words. Write the letters.**

Fruit and Vegetables	Dairy	Meat
a p p les	m i lk	c h i c k e n
on i o n s	e g g s	g r ound b e ef
p o ta t o e s		

Demonstrate by circling the first item on the board or overhead projector. Then have students complete the exercise in pairs. Correct the activity on the board or overhead projector and have students read the answers aloud.

6. Help students read the directions. Then present the listening. See "Presenting Listenings" on page vii. Check students' work. Ask volunteers to read the correct answers aloud.

About You **7.** Help students read the directions. Demonstrate by completing the first item on the board or overhead projector. Then have students complete the activity in pairs. Circulate to assist as needed. Ask volunteers to read the answers aloud.

Then check students' work yourself.

FOLLOW-UP

Where Is It? Arrange students in small groups. Provide each group with a set of word cards for food. Have them sort the cards by supermarket section. Have students say which food items they put in each section.

♦ Ask them to write lists of the food in each section. Write the names of the new food items on the board or overhead projector to help students spell them correctly. Have a student in each group read the group's lists aloud.

Identify kinds of food

Identify kinds of food packaging

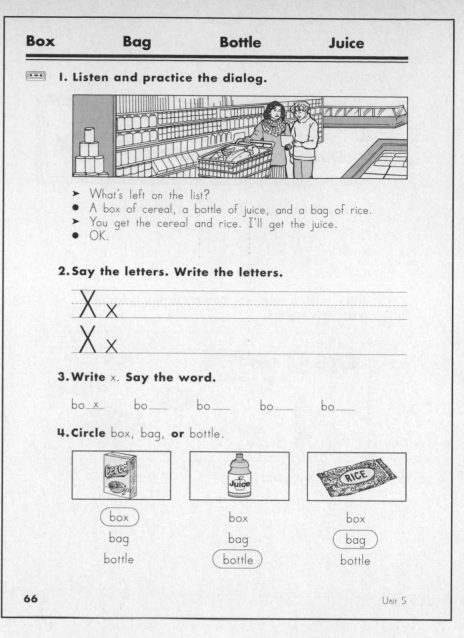

PREPARATION

Preteach the new language in the lesson. Follow these suggestions.

● Use picture cards, real food packages, and word cards to preteach the recognition words **box, bag, bottle,** and **juice.** See "Presenting Recognition Words" on page vii.

● Preteach the dialog. Write this shopping list on the board or overhead projector: **potatoes, apples, eggs, box of cereal, bottle of juice, bag of rice.** Identify what you've written as a **list.** Have students repeat the word. Then read the items aloud and place a picture of each or the realia food on display. Pick up the potatoes, put them in a basket or bag, and cross **potatoes** off the list. Repeat with the apples and the eggs.

Then ask, *What's left on the list?* Have students repeat. Say, *I'll get the juice.* Pick up the bottle of juice and add it to the groceries in your bag or basket. Then ask a volunteer to get the cereal and rice. Help him or her carry out your request.

PRESENTATION

1. Focus attention on the illustration. Help students identify the people, the place, and the food they see. Have them say as much as they can about the illustration. You may want to cue students by indicating items for them to name or by saying names of items and having students indicate them. Restate students' ideas in acceptable English and write them on the board or overhead projector.

Present the dialog. See "Presenting Dialogs" on page vii.

2. Present or review the letter **x.** See "Presenting Letters" on page vii. Then have students complete the activity. For additional reinforcement, use pages 3 and 10 of the Introductory Unit.

3. Help students read the directions. Demonstrate by completing the first item on the board or overhead projector. Then have students complete the exercise independently. Check students' work. Ask volunteers to read the word aloud and match it to a picture card.

4. Help students read the directions. Demonstrate by completing the first item on the board or overhead projector. Then have students complete

Real-Life English

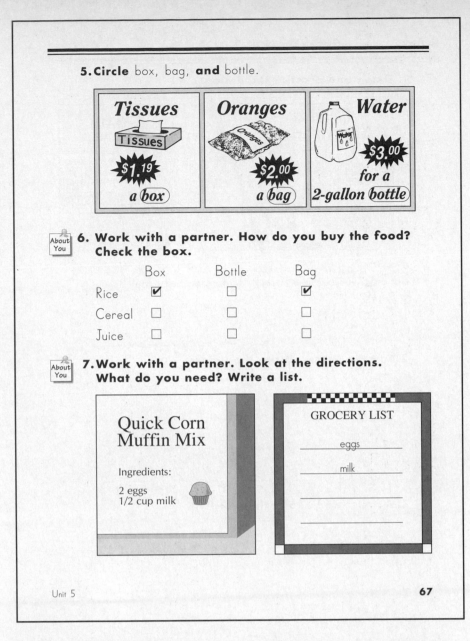

5. Circle box, bag, **and** bottle.

Tissues
Tissues
$1.19
a (box)

Oranges
$2.00
a (bag)

Water
$3.00
for a
2-gallon (bottle)

6. Work with a partner. How do you buy the food? Check the box.

	Box	Bottle	Bag
Rice	☑	☐	☑
Cereal	☐	☐	☐
Juice	☐	☐	☐

7. Work with a partner. Look at the directions. What do you need? Write a list.

Quick Corn
Muffin Mix

Ingredients:

2 eggs
1/2 cup milk

GROCERY LIST

eggs

milk

the exercise independently. Check students' work. Then ask volunteers to say the answers aloud.

5. Help students read the directions. Demonstrate by circling the first item on the board or overhead projector. Then have students complete the exercise independently. Correct the exercise on the board or overhead projector.

6. Help students read the directions. Demonstrate by completing the first item on the board or overhead projector. Then have students complete the activity in pairs. Correct the exercise on the board or overhead projector and ask volunteers to read the answers aloud.

7. First, teach the words **muffin** and **mix** by holding up a box of

muffin mix and a real muffin or a picture of a muffin. Then help students read the directions. Demonstrate by writing the first item on the board or overhead projector. Have students complete the activity in pairs. Ask volunteers to read their lists aloud.

FOLLOW UP

Box, Bag, or Bottle: With the class, brainstorm a list of food. Write the list on the board or overhead projector. Then ask students to tell you if they buy the food in a bag, a bottle, and/or a box.

♦ Have pairs of students copy the list from the board or overhead projector, then write the word **bag, bottle,** and/or **box** next to each item. Have

students come forward, one at a time, to write the name of the container(s) next to each item on the board.

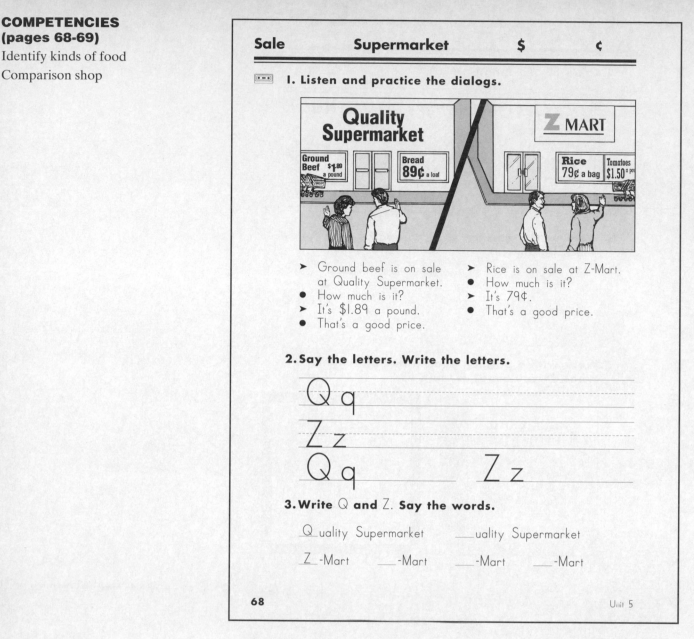

PREPARATION

Preteach the new language in the lesson. Follow these suggestions.

● Use picture cards and word cards, dollar bills, coins, Blackline Master 5: Money, and real supermarket ads or flyers to preteach **sale, supermarket,** and the symbols **$** and **¢.** See "Presenting Recognition Words" on page vii.

● Review U.S. currency. One at a time, display a quarter, dime, nickel, and penny and write **25¢, 10¢, 5¢,** and **1¢** on the board or overhead projector. (Or use Blackline Master 5: Money.) Say the amounts aloud and have students repeat. Show coins in various combinations and say and write the totals. Repeat with bills. Then write prices on the board or

overhead projector and have students count out the amounts in play money.

● Preteach the dialogs. Use the illustration on this page to teach the names of the two stores. To teach the word **pound,** draw a simple scale on the board or overhead projector. On the scale, draw a package of ground beef. Say, *A pound of ground beef.* Have students repeat. Hold up an item that weighs a pound, such as a pound box of cookies, and say, *This is one pound of (item).* Pass the item around so students can get a sense of how much it weighs. To teach **price,** display a supermarket ad or flyer, point to various prices, and say, *This is the price of (item).* Have students repeat. Write **pound** and **price** on the

board or overhead projector.

On the board or overhead projector write **Ground Beef $2.10 a pound.** Then write **Today: Ground beef $1.89 a pound.** Read what you've written. Then say, *Ground beef is on sale today.*

PRESENTATION

1. Focus attention on the illustration. Help students identify the stores, signs, and people. Have them say as much as they can about the illustration. You may want to cue students by indicating items for them to name or by saying names of items and having students indicate them. Restate students' ideas in acceptable English and write them on the board or overhead projector.

4. Write the amounts.

two dollars	$2.00
twenty cents	20¢
seventy-nine cents	79¢
a dollar sixty-nine	$1.69

5. Circle $, ¢, Sale, Supermarket, Eggs, Juice, Ground Beef, **and** Bread.

On Sale at **Quality Supermarket** This Week

| Eggs **89¢** a carton | Bread **99¢** a loaf | Juice **$1**²⁹ a bottle | Onions **50¢** a pound |
| Ground Beef **$1**⁸⁹ a pound | | | Tomatoes **$1**⁹⁹ a pound |

6. Work with a partner. Look at 5. Write the price.

| $1.99 | $1.89 | 99¢ | 89¢ |

Present the dialogs in turn. See "Presenting Dialogs" on page vii.

2. Present or review the letters **q** and **z.** See "Presenting Letters" on page vii. Then have students complete the activity. For additional reinforcement, use pages 3 and 10 of the Introductory Unit.

3. Help students read the directions. Demonstrate by completing the first item on the board or overhead projector. Then have students complete the exercise independently. Ask volunteers to read the words aloud and indicate them on the illustration on this page.

4. Help students read the directions. Demonstrate by completing the first item on the board or overhead projector. Then have students complete

the exercise independently. Have volunteers come forward one at a time to write the correct amounts on the board or overhead projector. Then check students' work.

5. Help students read the directions. Demonstrate by circling the first item on the board or overhead projector. Then have students complete the exercise. Correct the exercise on the board or overhead projector.

6. Help students read the directions. Demonstrate by completing the first item on the board or overhead projector. Then have students complete the activity in pairs. Ask volunteers to read the answers aloud. Write the answers on the board or overhead projector.

FOLLOW-UP

What's on Sale? Provide supermarket ads or flyers for each pair of students. Have them circle names of items they know. Have pairs of students hold up their ads and say the circled items aloud.

♦ Have each pair of students write a list of the items they circled and their prices. Ask volunteers to read their lists to the class.

◆ **Put It Together**

I. Work with a partner. Look at the pictures. What do you want? Write a list.

Z-MART This Week **SALE**

Juice $1.59 a bottle
Rice 79¢ a bag
Tomatoes $1.50 a pound
Chicken $1.29 a pound
Cereal
Eggs 79¢ a carton
Cereal $2.29 a box

SALE Quality Supermarket SALE THIS WEEK

Eggs 89¢ a carton
Bread
Ground Beef $1.89 a pound
Bread 99¢ a loaf
Juice $1.29 a bottle
Onions 50¢ a pound
Tomatoes $1.99 a pound

▪▪▪▪▪ Grocery List ▪▪▪▪▪

2. Where will you go? Circle the supermarket.

Quality Supermarket   Z-Mart

70   Unit 5

PREPARATION

On the board or overhead projector, write the words **chicken, juice, cereal, tomatoes, eggs, bag of rice, ground beef, onions, bread, supermarket,** and **list,** and the symbols **$** and **¢.** Ask volunteers to say the words aloud and find a picture card, realia item, or illustration in their books to match each one.

PRESENTATION

1. Help students read the directions. Ask them to say as much about the sales flyers as they can. Then demonstrate making a list by completing the first item on the board or overhead projector. Have students work in pairs to help each other complete the lists. Circulate to assist as need-

ed. When students have completed their lists, ask volunteers to write them on the board or overhead projector and read them aloud. Check students' lists.

2. Help students read the directions. Demonstrate on the board or overhead projector. Have students complete the exercise independently. Then name each supermarket and ask students to raise their hands if they circled it. Encourage students to explain their choices. Restate their ideas in acceptable English.

FOLLOW-UP

Your Favorite Store: Ask students where they shop. Write the names of the stores on the board or overhead projector. Arrange students in pairs

and have them help each other make a shopping list of items in their favorite stores. Circulate to assist as needed. Ask volunteers to write their lists on the board or overhead projector and read them aloud.

◆ Refer to the lists on the board or overhead projector. Ask, *What is a good price for (food item)?* As students suggest prices, write them next to the items or ask volunteers to come forward, one at a time, and write the prices.

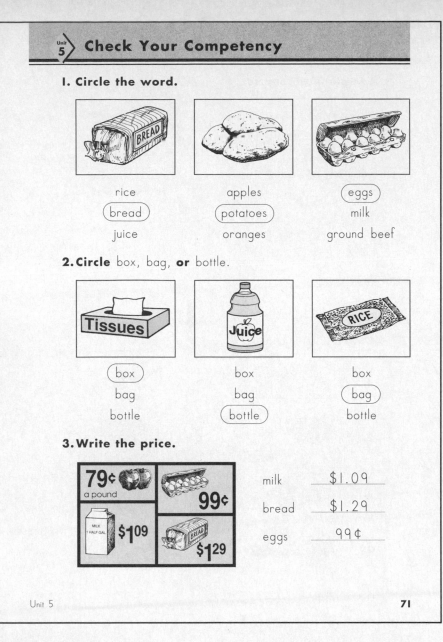

Check Your Competency

1. Circle the word.

rice	apples	(eggs)
(bread)	(potatoes)	milk
juice	oranges	ground beef

2. Circle box, bag, or bottle.

(box)	box	box
bag	bag	(bag)
bottle	(bottle)	bottle

3. Write the price.

79¢ a pound
99¢
$1⁰⁹
$1²⁹

milk $1.09

bread $1.29

eggs   99¢

PREPARATION

Briefly review the new language in this unit before students open their books. Write the words on the board or overhead projector and ask volunteers to find the matching picture cards or to indicate appropriate illustrations in their books. Review writing prices in dollars and cents.

Provide specific help as needed until you are sure students feel confident that they know all the new language.

PRESENTATION

Use any of the procedures in "Evaluation," page viii, with these pages. Record individuals' results on the Unit 5 Individual Competency Chart. Record the class's results on the Class Cumulative Competency Chart.

ENGLISH IN ACTION

An Optional Cooperative Learning Activity: Designate areas of the classroom to represent supermarket sections for Meat, Fruit and Vegetables, and Dairy. Make a sign for each section. Place picture cards and/or real food in the appropriate sections. Have students count off by twos. Ask the "ones" to be clerks. Provide tags and ask them to put prices on the food. Ask the remaining students to be shoppers. They will move around and ask clerks for locations of various items and for the prices of the items. Have the shoppers use play money from Blackline Master 5 to "pay" for their food. Have students change roles and repeat the activity. As an extension of this activity, you might want to arrange a visit to a nearby supermarket.

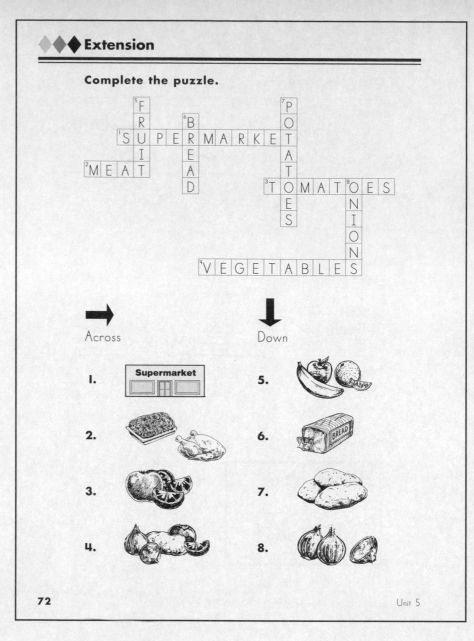

PREPARATION

With students, brainstorm a list of all the words they've learned in this unit. Write them on the board or overhead projector and read them aloud. Ask volunteers to find corresponding picture cards or pictures in the book.

PRESENTATION

Help students read the directions. Point out and read the word **across.** Demonstrate by completing the first word across on the board or overhead projector. Emphasize that there is one letter per square. Repeat with **down.** Then have students complete the activity in pairs. Circulate among them to assist as needed. Correct the activity on the board or overhead projector. Then check students' work yourself.

Unit

6 Shopping

ALDEN'S SHOES   SPORTSWORLD   FABER'S Department Store

Look at the picture.

Where are the people?

What are they doing?

73

Unit 6 Overview

UNIT COMPETENCIES

1. Identify kinds of clothes
2. Ask how much something costs
3. Understand amounts of money
4. Read size tags, price tags, and receipts
5. Write checks
6. Ask to return something

Unit 6 Optional Materials

● Word cards for **cash, check, charge, dollar, cents, driver's license, ID, receipt,** and the symbols **$** and **¢.**

● Pictures of clothes (or real clothes) in the unit (coat, sweater, shirt, shoes, socks, pants).

● Realia: A variety of coins, bills, and credit cards; a driver's license or other form of ID, checks, and receipts from various stores.

♦ Blackline Master 5: Money, page 146 and Blackline Master 6: Blank Check, page 147.

COMPETENCIES (page 73)

Identify kinds of clothes

PRESENTATION

Teaching Note: Use this page to warm up students, to check and draw on their prior knowledge, and to spark interest.

Read the unit title and questions aloud. Encourage students to identify as many places, people, and items in the picture as they can and to describe what is happening. As students may be able to say very little, you might have to prompt them by indicating items for them to name or by saying names of items and having students indicate them. Repeat students' ideas or restate them in

acceptable English. Model any words students do not know.

FOLLOW-UP

Where Can You Buy That? One at a time, show students a variety of items they could buy in the stores in the illustration on this page, such as a tennis racket, a pair of shoes, a sweater, a box of tissues, a hat, etc. Model any words students want to know. Ask volunteers to name each item and indicate the store or stores in which they could purchase each one.

♦ Arrange students in pairs. Have them refer to the illustration. Ask them to point out to each other stores they would like to shop in and name items they would like to buy

there. Model any words students want to know. Have each student tell the class an item his or her partner wants to buy.

Identify kinds of clothes

Ask how much something costs

Understand amounts of money

Read size tags, price tags, and receipts

Cash   Charge

▭ I. Listen and practice the dialogs.

> ➤ How much are these shoes?
> ● They're $20.00.
> ➤ I'll take them.
> ● Cash or charge?
> ➤ Charge.

> ➤ How much is this shirt?
> ● It's $8.00.
> ➤ I'll take it.
> ● Cash or charge?
> ➤ Cash.

2. Say the names of the clothes.

a. sweater   **b.** coat   **c.** pants   **d.** socks

3. Say the words. Write the words.

cash   charge

_____   _____

_____   _____

_____   _____

74   Unit 6

PREPARATION

Preteach the new language in the lesson. Follow these suggestions.

● Use word cards, real credit cards, and real coins and bills (or Blackline Master 5: Money) to preteach the recognition words **cash** and **charge.** See "Presenting Recognition Words" on page vii.

● Review money. Follow the instructions on page 68.

● Use pictures and/or real clothes to teach the words **sweater, shirt, coat, shoes, pants,** and **socks.** Focus attention on each item or picture, say the name, and have students repeat. Then ask volunteers, one at a time, to indicate an item and name it.

● Preteach the first dialog. Display pictures of a sweater, shirt, coat, shoes, pants, and socks or display the real items. Label the shirt $8.00. Label the shoes $20.00. Look at the pictures or items and say, *How much is the shirt? It's $8.00.* Have students repeat. Pick up the picture or the real shirt and say, *I'll take it.* Have students repeat.

PRESENTATION

1. Focus attention on the illustration. Help students identify the people, the sections of the store, and the items for sale. Have them say as much as they can about the illustration. You may want to cue students by indicating items for them to name or by saying names of items and having students indicate them. Restate students' ideas in acceptable English and write them on the board or overhead projector.

Present the dialogs in turn. See "Presenting Dialogs" on page vii.

2. Help students read the directions. Model each word in turn and have students repeat. Then have students in pairs say the names of the clothes to each other. Have students change partners and repeat the exercise. Circulate to assist as needed. Ask volunteers to say the names of the clothes aloud.

3. Help students read the directions. Demonstrate by completing the first item on the board or overhead projector. Then have students complete the exercise independently. Check students' work.

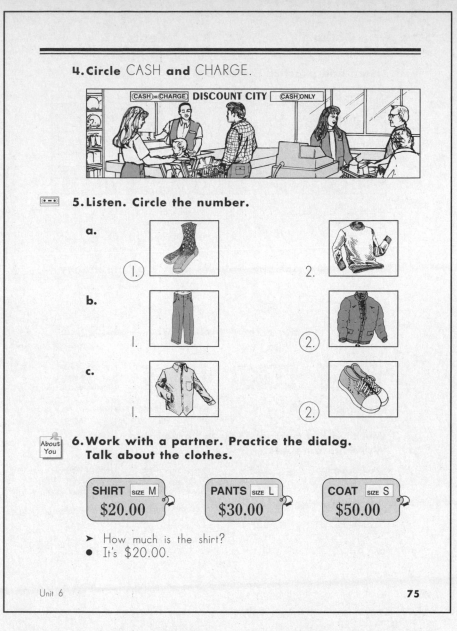

4. Circle CASH and CHARGE.

5. Listen. Circle the number.

a.
   (1.)   2.

b.
   1.   (2.)

c.
   1.   (2.)

6. Work with a partner. Practice the dialog. Talk about the clothes.

SHIRT SIZE M	PANTS SIZE L	COAT SIZE S
$20.00	$30.00	$50.00

➤ How much is the shirt?
● It's $20.00.

4. Help students read the directions. Demonstrate by completing the first item on the board or overhead projector. Have students complete the exercise independently. Correct the exercise on the board or overhead projector. Check students' work.

5. Help students read the directions. Then present the listening. See "Presenting Listenings" on page vii. Ask volunteers to read their correct answers aloud.

6. Review the dialog with the class. Help students identify the items. Then have students ask and answer the question in the dialog in pairs, switching roles several times. Have students change partners and repeat the exercise. Circulate to assist as needed. Have several pairs say the dialog aloud for the class.

FOLLOW-UP

I'll Take It: Provide each pair of students with a clothing store flyer or newspaper advertisement that illustrates items students are familiar with. Have students continue using the dialog in item 6, referring this time to items in the advertisements. Circulate to assist as needed. Model any words students want to know. Ask volunteers to repeat their conversations for the class.

♦ Have pairs of students swap flyers. This time have students use the dialog on page 74 as they refer to the flyer or newspaper advertisements. Model any words students want to know. Ask volunteers to repeat their conversations for the class.

Identify kinds of clothes

Ask how much something costs

Understand amounts of money

Read size tags, price tags, and receipts

PREPARATION

Preteach the new language in the lesson. Follow these suggestions.

● To teach the words **penny, nickel, dime,** and **quarter,** use real coins and bills or Blackline Master 5: Money. Focus attention on each coin or bill, identify it, and have students repeat.

● Use word cards and real bills and coins and/or Blackline Master 5: Money to preteach the recognition words **dollar** and **cents** and the symbols **$** and **¢.** See "Presenting Recognition Words" on page vii.

● Preteach the dialog. Display a picture of a TV or draw a picture on the board or overhead projector. Help students identify the TV. Label the TV with a price tag of $65.50. Ask,

How much is the TV? Prompt the class to answer, *It's $65.50.* Say, *I'll take it.* Have students repeat.

PRESENTATION

1. Focus attention on the illustration. Help students identify the type of store and the items. Have them say as much as they can about the illustration. You may want to cue students by indicating items for them to name or by saying names of items and having students indicate them. Restate students' ideas in acceptable English and write them on the board or overhead projector.

Present the dialog. See "Presenting Dialogs" on page vii.

2. Help students read the directions.

Demonstrate by reading the name of each item in turn. Have students repeat. Then have students in pairs say the names of the coins and bills aloud to each other. Have them change partners and repeat the activity. Circulate to assist as needed. Ask volunteers to say the names of the bills and coins aloud.

3. Help students read the directions. Demonstrate by completing the first item on the board or overhead projector. Then have students work in pairs, saying and writing the amounts of money. Ask volunteers to write the correct answers on the board or overhead projector. Check students' work.

4. Help students read the directions.

4. Circle NICKELS, DIMES, QUARTERS, **and** DOLLAR.

5. Listen. Circle the amount you hear.

a. $21.98   ($21.99) $29.00

b. $15.01 $15.10   ($15.00)

c. 85¢ $85.00   ($8.50)

6. Work with a partner. Practice the dialog. Talk about the items.

$11.95 $1.25 $89.95

➤ How much is the shirt?
● It's $11.95.
➤ I'll take it.

Demonstrate by completing the first item on the board or overhead projector. Then have students complete the exercise independently. Correct the exercise on the board or overhead projector.

5. Help students read the directions. Then present the listening. See "Presenting Listenings" on page vii. Ask volunteers to read their answers aloud.

6. Review the dialog with the class. Help students identify the items. Then have students say the dialog in pairs, switching roles several times. Have students change partners and repeat the exercise. Have several pairs of students say the dialog aloud for the class.

FOLLOW-UP

How Much Is It? Provide each student with a picture of an item or a real item such as a sweater, notebook, book, pencil, etc. Ask the student to write a price for the item on a tag and attach it to the item. Then arrange students in pairs to ask and answer the question, *How much is the (item)?* Have students change partners several times and repeat the activity. Circulate to assist as needed. Have volunteers say their conversations aloud.

♦ Repeat the activity, but provide each student with play money. Use Blackline Master 5: Money. This time, ask students to buy the items and pay their partners for them.

Check to make sure each student has paid the correct amount of money.

Ask how much something costs

Understand amounts of money

Write checks

Driver's License   ID   Check

I. Listen and practice the dialog.

➤ Cash, check, or charge?
● Check.
➤ OK. Please show me some ID.
● Here's my driver's license.

**2. Work with a partner. Look at the check.
Answer the questions.**

Ana Soto   581
386 Ocean Avenue
Long Beach, CA   DATE *January 31, 1995*

PAY TO THE
ORDER OF   *Northwest Hardware* $ *32.50*

Thirty-two and 50/100   DOLLARS

✳ **CAL**BANK   *Ana Soto*

a. How much is the check for?____$32.50____

b. What store is the check to?_Northwest Hardware_

3. Write the amounts for a check.

a. $15.95 _Fifteen and 95/100_____ DOLLARS

b. $21.50 _Twenty-one and 50/100_____ DOLLARS

c. $3.75 _Three and 75/100_____ DOLLARS

78   Unit 6

PREPARATION

Preteach the new language in the lesson. Follow these suggestions.

● To teach the concept of a check, show students a real check (or use Blackline Master 6). Explain that people can use checks instead of cash to pay for things.

● Use real items and word cards to preteach the recognition words **driver's license, ID,** and **check.** See "Presenting Recognition Words" on page vii.

● Explain that the dollar amounts on a check are written in words. Then teach students to write numbers **1** through **100** in words. Write a numeral on the board or overhead projector, have a student read it

aloud, and write the word for the number on the board or overhead projector.

Teaching Note: You may wish to teach students to write numbers in words over the course of several days rather than all at once.

● Preteach the dialog. To teach the word **show,** give a series of commands such as **Show me a pencil, show me a book, show me a penny,** and pantomime each command as you say it. Then repeat and have individuals respond by showing you objects. Then say, *Please show me some ID.* Have students show you their IDs.

Place a book on your desk and ask a volunteer to pretend to buy it. Ask, *Cash, check, or charge?* Have stu-

dents repeat. Prompt the volunteer to answer, *Check.* Say *OK. Please show me some ID.*

PRESENTATION

1. Focus attention on the illustration and have students say as much as they can about it. You may want to cue students by indicating items for them to name or by saying names of items and having students indicate them. Restate students' ideas in acceptable English and write them on the board or overhead projector.

Present the dialog. See "Presenting Dialogs" on page vii.

2. Help students read the directions. Point out how much the check is for and to whom it is written. Refer to

4. Circle CHECK, checks, ID, **and** driver's license.

Discount CITY
Customer Service

STORE CHECK POLICY

1. No out-of-state checks.
2. Name and address on checks.
3. A driver's license or another form of ID.

5. Write a check to Northwest Hardware for $34.78.

226

DATE _____

PAY TO THE
ORDER OF Northwest Hardware $ 34.78

Thirty-four and 78/100   DOLLARS

✳ CALBANK   _____

the picture to illustrate a hardware store. Help students read the questions. Then have them complete the exercise in pairs. Ask volunteers to write the answers on the board or overhead projector and read them aloud. Check students' work.

3. Help students read the directions. Demonstrate by completing the first item on the board or overhead projector. Then have students complete the exercise. Circulate to assist as needed. Ask volunteers to write the answers on the board or overhead projector. Check students' work.

4. Help students read the directions. Demonstrate by completing the first item on the board or overhead projector. Have students complete the exercise independently. Correct the

exercise on the board or overhead projector. Then check students' work.

5. Help students read the directions. Draw a check on the board or overhead projector. Demonstrate filling in the check. Then have students complete the exercise independently. Ask a volunteer to fill in the check on the board or overhead projector. Check students' work.

FOLLOW-UP

Paying by Check: Provide students with blank checks. Use Blackline Master 6: Blank Check. Ask students what they might pay for by check (rent, gas, phone, etc.) and approximate amounts they might pay for

each one. Write the business names and money amounts on the board or overhead projector so students can refer to them. Then have them work in pairs to write checks to these businesses. Circulate to assist as needed.

♦ Have students write additional checks for other bills they want to pay by check.

Receipt

🎞 **I. Listen and practice the dialog.**

➤ I want to return this chair.
● Give me the receipt, please.
➤ Here.

2. Answer the questions.

a. What is he returning? _a chair_

b. Does he have the receipt? _yes_

3. Look at the receipts. Circle the totals.

```
SHOP 'N SAVE MARKETS
8040 MESA DRIVE

  LARGE ORANGES   $ .10
  APPLES            .69
  JUICE            1.35
  MILK             1.35
  BREAD            1.29
            TOTAL  $4.78
```

```
24-HOUR DELI

  MILK          $1.25
  SANDWICH       4.00

      TOTAL    $5.25
```

80   Unit 6

PREPARATION

Preteach the new language in the lesson. Follow these suggestions.

● Use the picture card, the word card, and real receipts to preteach the recognition word **receipt.** See "Presenting Recognition Words" on page vii.

● Preteach the dialog. To teach **return,** give a student some play money and pretend to buy the student's book. Step back, look through the book, and say, *I don't want this book. I want to return it.* Take the book back to the student and exchange it for the money.

PRESENTATION

1. Focus attention on the illustration.

Help students identify the type of store and the items. Have them say as much as they can about the illustration. You may want to cue students by indicating items for them to name or by saying names of items and having students indicate them. Restate students' ideas in acceptable English and write them on the board or overhead projector.

Present the dialog. See "Presenting Dialogs" on page vii.

2. Help students read the directions and the questions. Demonstrate by completing the first item on the board or overhead projector. Have students complete the exercise. Then ask volunteers to read their answers to the class. Correct students' work.

3. Help students read the directions.

Demonstrate by circling the first total on the board or overhead projector. Then have students complete the exercise independently. Ask volunteers to write the totals on the board or overhead projector and read them aloud.

4. Help students read the directions. Demonstrate by completing the first item on the board or overhead projector. Then have students complete the exercise independently. Ask volunteers to come forward, one at a time, and match the items on the board or overhead projector. Check students' work.

FOLLOW-UP

Reading Receipts: Provide an itemized receipt to each pair of students.

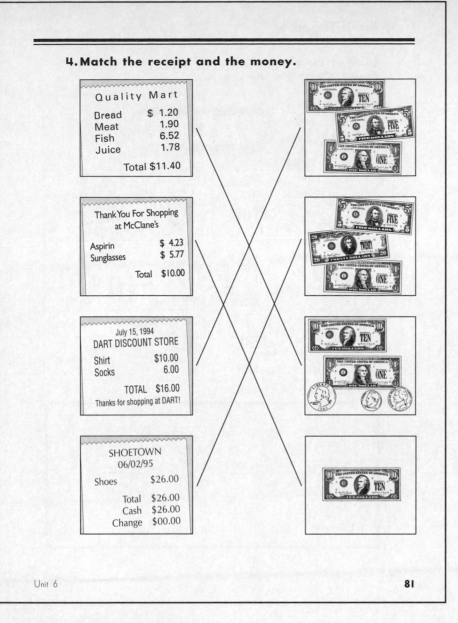

4. Match the receipt and the money.

Quality Mart

Dread	$ 1.20
Meat	1.90
Fish	6.52
Juice	1.78
Total	$11.40

ThankYou For Shopping
at McClane's

Aspirin	$ 4.23
Sunglasses	$ 5.77
Total	$10.00

July 15, 1994
DART DISCOUNT STORE

Shirt	$10.00
Socks	6.00
TOTAL	$16.00

Thanks for shopping at DART!

SHOETOWN
06/02/95

Shoes	$26.00
Total	$26.00
Cash	$26.00
Change	$00.00

Unit 6   **81**

On the board, write: **What did they buy? What is the total?** and **Cash, check or charge?** Have students discuss the receipts and figure what was bought, what the total amount paid was, and whether the payment was by cash, check, or charge. Ask volunteers to tell the class about their receipts.

♦ Provide each pair of students with a blank check. Use Blackline Master 6. Ask them to write a check to the store for the total amount of the receipt. Check students' work.

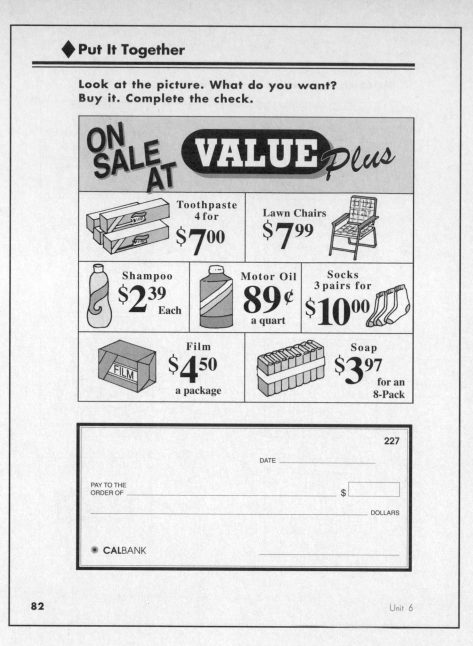

◆ Put It Together

Look at the picture. What do you want?
Buy it. Complete the check.

ON SALE AT VALUE *Plus*

Toothpaste 4 for $7.00	Lawn Chairs $7.99
Shampoo $2.39 Each	Motor Oil 89¢ a quart
	Socks 3 pairs for $10.00
Film $4.50 a package	Soap $3.97 for an 8-Pack

227

DATE _____

PAY TO THE ORDER OF _____ $ [____]

_____ DOLLARS

✷ **CAL**BANK _____

82   Unit 6

PREPARATION

On the board or overhead projector, write the words **dollars, cents,** and **check**. Ask volunteers to read the words aloud and find a matching illustration in the book for each.

PRESENTATION

Help students read the directions. Focus attention on the illustration and discuss it with students. Model any words students want to know. Demonstrate by choosing the item you wish to buy and filling out a blank check for the correct amount on the board or overhead projector. Then have students complete the exercise independently. Encourage students to share their choices with the class. Ask volunteers to show

their checks to the rest of the class. Then check students' work.

FOLLOW-UP

Cashing Checks: Using Blackline Master 6: Blank Check, demonstrate how to endorse a check. Explain that students will need to endorse checks in order to deposit them or to cash them (exchange them for money). Then provide each student with a blank check and arrange students in pairs. Instruct each student to write a check to his or her partner for any amount under $100 and then give the check to his or her partner. Ask students to endorse the checks they received. Check to make sure students have endorsed their checks correctly.

♦ Ask a volunteer to play the role of a banker. Have students come forward to the "bank" one at a time and exchange their endorsed checks for bills and coins. Suggest that students carefully count the money they receive to verify that it is the correct amount. Then check the amounts yourself.

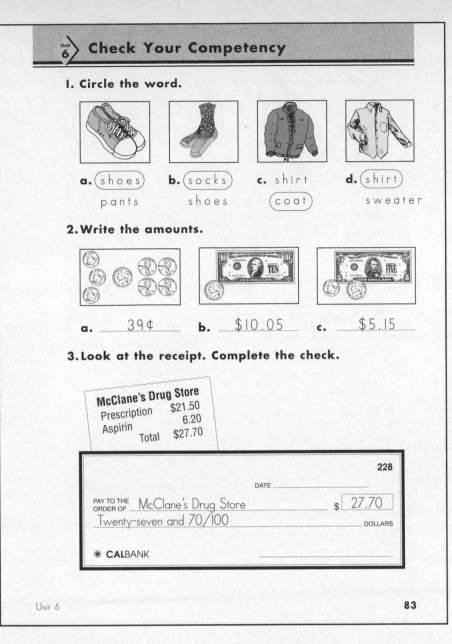

1. Circle the word.

a. (shoes)
pants

b. (socks)
shoes

c. shirt
(coat)

d. (shirt)
sweater

2. Write the amounts.

a. 39¢

b. $10.05

c. $5.15

3. Look at the receipt. Complete the check.

McClane's Drug Store
Prescription $21.50
Aspirin   6.20
        Total $27.70

228

DATE _____

PAY TO THE
ORDER OF McClane's Drug Store $ 27.70

Twenty-seven and 70/100 _____ DOLLARS

✹ CALBANK

Unit 6   **83**

PREPARATION

Briefly review the new language in this unit before students open their books. Write the words on the board or overhead projector and ask volunteers to find matching word cards and picture cards or real items. Review amounts of money and how to write a check.

Review the spelling of **one, eight, ten, twenty, thirty, forty,** and **fifty.**

Provide specific help as needed until you are sure students feel confident that they know all the new language.

PRESENTATION

Use any of the procedures in "Evaluation," page viii, with these pages. Record individuals' results on the Unit 6 Individual Competency Chart. Record the class's results on the Class Cumulative Competency Chart.

ENGLISH IN ACTION

An Optional Cooperative Learning Activity: Set up drug stores at several stations around the classroom. At each, place pictures or realia of common items you can purchase in a drug store, such as a box of tissues, notebook, a comb, film, a candy bar, etc. Label each item with a price tag. Ask for volunteers to be salesclerks at the stations. Ask the rest of the students to be shoppers. Provide shoppers with play money and blank checks. Use Blackline Masters 5 and 6. Have the shoppers select items

and wait in the check-out line to "pay" for them by cash or check. Tell the shoppers they can get back in line to return items or make additional purchases if they wish. Repeat with different students as salesclerks. As an extension of this activity, you might wish to take your class on a visit to a nearby drug store.

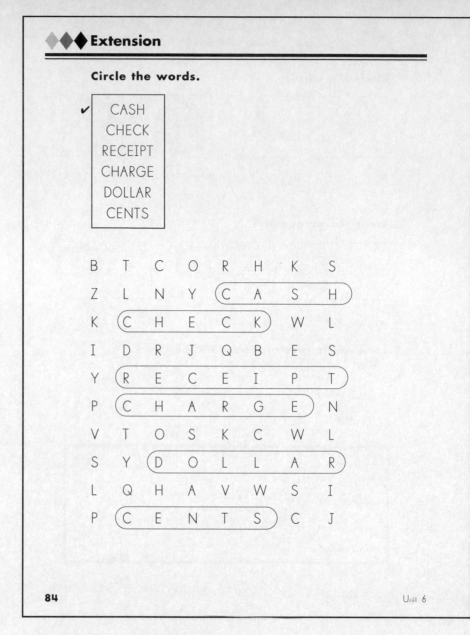

◆◆◆ Extension

Circle the words.

✔
- CASH
- CHECK
- RECEIPT
- CHARGE
- DOLLAR
- CENTS

```
B  T  C  O  R  H  K  S
Z  L  N  Y (C  A  S  H)
K (C  H  E  C  K) W  L
I  D  R  J  Q  B  E  S
Y (R  E  C  E  I  P  T)
P (C  H  A  R  G  E) N
V  T  O  S  K  C  W  L
S  Y (D  O  L  L  A  R)
L  Q  H  A  V  W  S  I
P (C  E  N  T  S) C  J
```

PREPARATION

Write **CACASHCA** on the board in letters approximately the same size as those on the word card for **CASH.** Hold the word card against the first four letters on the board, shake your head, and say *No.* Move the card so it lines up with **ACAS** and repeat your rejection of the match. Move the card again so that it lines up with **CASH.** This time indicate your acceptance of the match.

PRESENTATION

Help students read the directions. Demonstrate by circling **CASH** on the board.

Have students complete the word puzzle activity in pairs. Circulate among them to assist as needed.

Copy the puzzle on the board or overhead projector. Have volunteers come forward, one at a time, to circle the correct answer for each item. Check students' work.

Look at the picture.

Where are the people?

What are they doing?

85

UNIT COMPETENCIES

1. Say where you live
2. Identify kinds of housing
3. Identify furniture and rooms
4. Read for-rent signs
5. Ask about the rent and the deposit

Unit 7 Optional Materials

● Picture cards and word cards for types of housing **(house, apartment),** rooms **(bedroom, kitchen, bathroom, living room)** and furniture **(bed, sofa, chair, lamp, refrigerator, stove, table).**

● Word cards for **rent** and **deposit.**

● Realia: Illustrated newspaper advertisements and/or flyers for apartments and houses.

♦ Blackline Master 5: Money, page 146, Blackline Master 6: Blank Check, page 147, Blackline Master 7a: Rooms, page 148, and Blackline Master 7b: Furniture, page 149.

COMPETENCIES (page 85)

Identify kinds of housing

Read for-rent signs

PRESENTATION

Teaching Note: Use this page to warm up students, to check and draw on their prior knowledge, and to spark interest.

Read the unit title and questions aloud. Encourage students to identify as many items in the picture as they can and to describe what the people are doing. As students may be able to say very little, you might have to prompt them by indicating items for them to name or by saying names of items and having students indicate them. Model any words students do not know. Repeat students' ideas or restate them in acceptable English.

FOLLOW-UP

What Do You Recognize? Provide pairs of students with magazines that include pictures of the interiors and/or exteriors of apartments and houses. Have students find pictures of items that are also in the illustration on this page and name them. Circulate to assist as needed. Model any words students want to know. Have pairs exchange magazines and repeat the activity. Ask volunteers to show pictures to the class and name items in the pictures.

♦ Have partners take turns indicating items in magazine pictures for the other to name. Then ask each student to tell the class an item his or her partner mentioned. Write the words on the board or overhead projector.

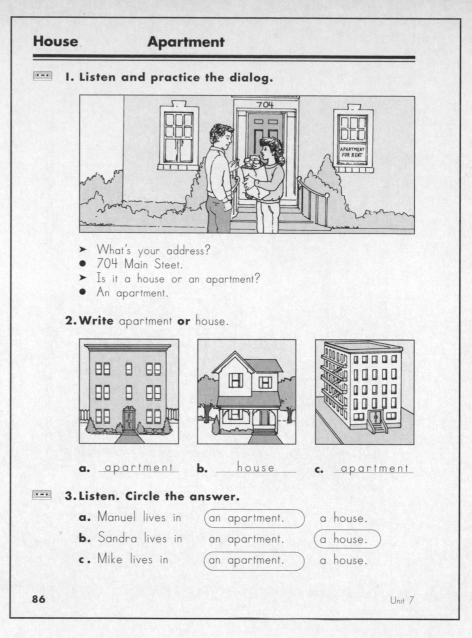

House   Apartment

🔲 **I. Listen and practice the dialog.**

➤ What's your address?
● 704 Main Steet.
➤ Is it a house or an apartment?
● An apartment.

2. Write apartment **or** house.

a. <u>apartment</u>   **b.** <u>house</u>   **c.** <u>apartment</u>

🔲 **3. Listen. Circle the answer.**

a. Manuel lives in (an apartment.) a house.
b. Sandra lives in   an apartment.   (a house.)
c. Mike lives in   (an apartment.) a house.

86   Unit 7

PREPARATION

Preteach the new language in the lesson. Follow these suggestions.

● Use picture cards and word cards to preteach the recognition words **house** and **apartment**. See "Presenting Recognition Words" on page vii.

Teaching Note: If necessary, preteach or review numerals **0** to **99.** See pages 4 and 10 of the Introductory Unit and page 56 of Unit 4. You might also teach the names of housing your students live in, such as **mobile home, garage apartment,** etc.

● Preteach the dialog. To review **address,** refer to page 16. Ask volunteers to say and write their addresses on the board or overhead projector.

Then point to the illustration at the top of this page and ask, *Is this a house or an apartment?* Have students repeat. Model the answer, *An apartment,* and have students repeat.

PRESENTATION

1. Focus attention on the illustration. Have students say as much as they can about it. You may want to cue students by indicating items for them to name or by saying names of items and having students indicate them. Restate students' ideas in acceptable English and write them on the board or overhead projector.

Present the dialog. See "Presenting Dialogs" on page vii.

2. Help students read the directions.

Demonstrate by completing the first item on the board or overhead projector. Then have students complete the exercise independently. Ask volunteers to write answers on the board or overhead projector and say them aloud. Check students' work.

3. Help students read the directions. Then present the listening. See "Presenting Listenings" on page vii. Ask volunteers to read the answers aloud.

4. Help students read the directions. Demonstrate by circling the first item on the board or overhead projector. Then have students complete the exercise. Ask volunteers to circle the answers on the board or overhead projector. Check students' work.

4. Circle house **and** apartment.

FOR RENT
2-bedroom (house)
Small yard—Nice neighborhood
Call Smith Realty
555-0984

For Rent
1-bedroom
(apartment)
Call Larry at
555-7672

5. Write your address. Write a house **or** an apartment.

a. My address is _____ .

b. I live in _____ .

6. Write the sentences in 5.

_____

_____

7. Work with a group. Complete the chart.

NAME	HOUSE	APARTMENT
Anna	✔	

5. Help students read the directions. Demonstrate by completing the items on the board or overhead projector with your (or a fictitious) address. Then have students complete the exercise. Ask volunteers to read their answers aloud. Check students' work.

Teaching Note: Throughout the unit, students should feel free to use real or fictitious information about their residences.

6. Help students read the directions. Demonstrate by completing the first item on the board or overhead projector. Then have students complete the exercise independently. Check students' work.

7. Help students read the directions. Demonstrate by asking two or three students if they live in houses or apartments and filling in the information on a chart on the board or overhead projector. Then arrange students in small groups to complete the activity. Circulate to assist as needed. Ask volunteers to read their groups' charts aloud.

FOLLOW-UP

Where Do We Live? On the board or overhead projector, complete the chart in item 7 for the entire class by having volunteers come forward in turn to ask their classmates questions and fill in sections of the chart. Then have students count the number of people that live in houses and apart-

ments. Write the totals at the bottom of the chart.

♦ Have students interview another class to complete a similar chart. Then have them tally and compare the numbers with those for their class.

Say where you live

Identify kinds of housing

Identify furniture and rooms

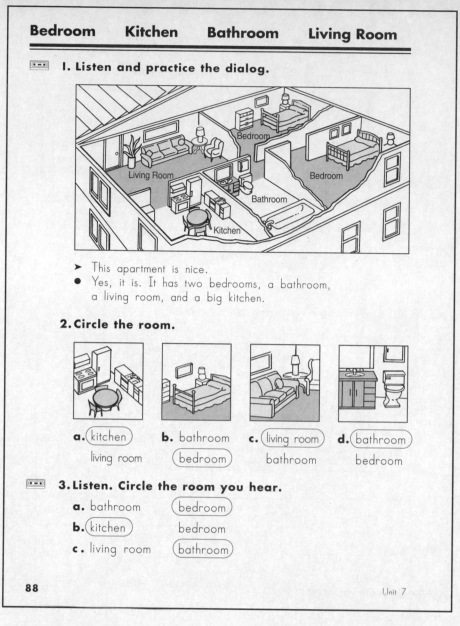

Bedroom   Kitchen   Bathroom   Living Room

1. Listen and practice the dialog.

> This apartment is nice.
● Yes, it is. It has two bedrooms, a bathroom, a living room, and a big kitchen.

2. Circle the room.

a. (kitchen)
   living room

b. bathroom
   (bedroom)

c. (living room)
   bathroom

d. (bathroom)
   bedroom

3. Listen. Circle the room you hear.

a. bathroom   (bedroom)

b. (kitchen)   bedroom

c. living room   (bathroom)

88   Unit 7

PREPARATION

Preteach the new language in the lesson. Follow these suggestions.

● Use picture cards and word cards, the illustration on the page, and Blackline Master 7a: Rooms, to preteach the recognition words **bedroom, kitchen, bathroom,** and **living room.** See "Presenting Recognition Words" on page vii.

● Preteach the dialog. To teach **big,** hold up pictures of two houses, one of which is big, the other small, and say of the larger one, *This house is big.* Have students repeat. Similarly, teach **nice.** Then have students show you realia or pictures of items that are big and/or nice.

PRESENTATION

1. Focus attention on the illustration. Help students identify the types of rooms and the number of each. Have them say as much as they can about the illustration. You may want to cue students by indicating items for them to name or by saying names of items and having students indicate them. Restate students' ideas in acceptable English and write them on the board or overhead projector.

Present the dialog. See "Presenting Dialogs" on page vii.

2. Help students read the directions. Demonstrate by completing the first item on the board or overhead projector. Have students complete the exercise independently. Ask volunteers to read their answers aloud.

Then check students' work.

3. Help students read the directions. Then present the listening. See "Presenting Listenings" on page vii. Ask volunteers to read the answers aloud.

4. Help students read the directions. Demonstrate by circling the first item on the board or overhead projector. Then have students complete the exercise. Ask volunteers to come forward one at a time to circle the answers on the board or overhead projector and match them with picture cards. Check students' work.

5. Help students read the directions. Demonstrate by completing the first item on the board or overhead projector. Have students complete the exercise independently. Ask volun-

4. Circle Kitchen, Bedroom, Bathroom, **and** Living Room.

Glenwood
APARTMENTS
One-Bedroom
Floor Plan

Dining Room — (Bathroom) — Closet — (Bedroom) — (Kitchen) — (Living Room)

5. Say the words. Write the words.

kitchen   bedroom   bathroom

_____   _____   _____

_____   _____   _____

_____   _____   _____

6. Work with a partner.
Write the rooms in your house or apartment.
Write the rooms in your partner's house
or apartment.

My House   **My Partner's House**

_____   _____

_____   _____

_____   _____

_____   _____

teers to write the words on the board or overhead projector, say them aloud, and match them with picture cards. Then check students' work.

6. Help students read the directions. Demonstrate by completing the first item on the board or overhead projector. Then have students complete the exercise in pairs. Circulate to assist as needed. Ask volunteers to write their answers on the board or overhead projector and read them aloud. Check students' work.

FOLLOW-UP

Naming Rooms: Provide each pair of students with a copy of Blackline Master 7a: Rooms. Ask students to write **house** or **apartment** under the picture. Then have them label the rooms. Sketch the house on the board or overhead projector and ask a volunteer to label the rooms. Check students' work.

♦ Designate areas of the classroom to be different rooms of a house by placing or taping picture cards for kitchen, bathroom, bedroom, and living room to the wall or floor. Ask a volunteer to walk to the correct room as you give a series of instructions, such as **Go to the kitchen, Go to the living room,** etc. Then ask a student to give instructions to another volunteer. Repeat until all students who want to have participated.

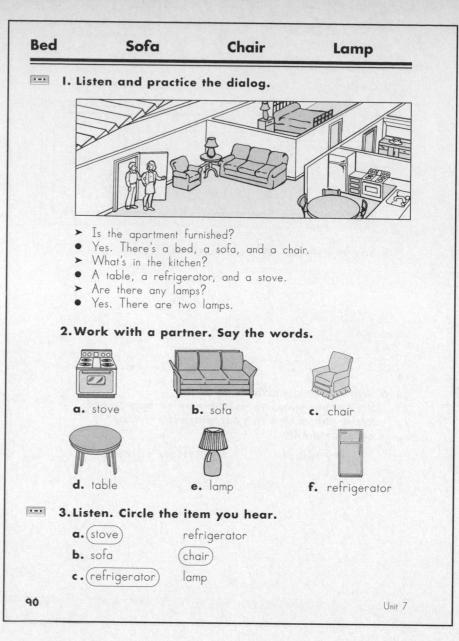

Bed   Sofa   Chair   Lamp

▰ **I. Listen and practice the dialog.**

➤ Is the apartment furnished?
● Yes. There's a bed, a sofa, and a chair.
➤ What's in the kitchen?
● A table, a refrigerator, and a stove.
➤ Are there any lamps?
● Yes. There are two lamps.

2. Work with a partner. Say the words.

a. stove   **b.** sofa   **c.** chair

d. table   **e.** lamp   **f.** refrigerator

▰ **3. Listen. Circle the item you hear.**

a. (stove)   refrigerator
b. sofa   (chair)
c. (refrigerator) lamp

90   Unit 7

PREPARATION

Preteach the new language in the lesson. Follow these suggestions.

● Use picture cards, word cards, the illustration on the page, and Blackline Master 7b: Furniture, to preteach the recognition words **bed, sofa, chair, lamp, refrigerator, stove,** and **table.** See "Presenting Recognition Words" on page vii.

● Preteach the dialog. To teach **furnished,** use Blackline Master 7a: Rooms and Blackline Master 7b: Furniture. First show the empty rooms and say, *The apartment isn't furnished.* Then add furniture to the rooms and say, *The apartment is furnished.* Have students repeat. Refer to the illustrations of apartments or houses in this unit and, for each, ask,

Is the (apartment) furnished? Have students repeat. Model the answer, *Yes, it is. There's (a bed, a sofa, and a chair).* Have students repeat.

PRESENTATION

1. Focus attention on the illustration. Have students say as much as they can about it. You may want to cue students by indicating items for them to name or by saying names of items and having students indicate them. Restate students' ideas in acceptable English and write them on the board or overhead projector.

Present the dialog. See "Presenting Dialogs" on page vii.

2. Help students read the directions. Demonstrate with a volunteer by

saying the names of the items to each other. Then have students complete the exercise in pairs. Circulate to assist as needed. Ask volunteers to say the words aloud to the class.

3. Help students read the directions. Then present the listening. See "Presenting Listenings" on page vii. Ask volunteers to read the correct answers aloud and match them to picture cards.

4. Help students read the directions. Demonstrate by circling the first item on the board or overhead projector. Then have students complete the exercise. Ask volunteers to circle the correct answers on the board or overhead projector. Check students' work.

5. Help students read the directions.

90   Real-Life English

4. Circle Lamps, Stoves, Sofas, Chairs, Tables, Beds, **and** Refrigerators.

Griffith's Presidents' Day SALE	All (Sofas) $329⁰⁰	(Refrigerators) $659⁰⁰	Gas and Electric (Stoves) $469⁵⁰
			Kitchen (Tables) $129⁹⁸
	Table (Lamps) $19⁹⁹	Dining Room (Chairs) $39⁵⁰	All (Beds) $89⁹⁹

5. Work with a partner. Write the words.

stove	sofa	bed	refrigerator

6. Look at the ad in 4. What do you want to buy? Make a list. Write the prices.

Item	Price
Lamp	$19.99

Unit 7   **91**

Demonstrate by completing the first item on the board or overhead projector. Have students complete the exercise in pairs. Ask volunteers to write the words on the board or overhead projector. Check students' work.

6. Help students read the directions. Demonstrate by writing a list of items you want to buy and their prices on the board or overhead projector. Then have students work in pairs to help each other make lists and write prices. Circulate to assist as needed. Have volunteers write their choices on the board. Check students' work.

Teaching Note: You might help students add up their purchases and then use Blackline Master 6: Blank Check to write checks to pay for their purchases.

FOLLOW-UP

Arranging Furniture: Have students work in pairs to take turns arranging the furniture in Blackline Master 7b in the rooms in Blackline Master 7a. Students should give each other directions on how to put furniture into the rooms. As they work, ask them to name the item of furniture and the room they are placing it in. Circulate to assist as needed. Ask volunteers to name the furniture they placed in each room.

♦ Provide pairs of students with magazines or newspaper ads that include pictures of different items of furniture. Have students find pic-

tures of items of furniture different from the ones they have already learned and that they would want in their own home. Then have students cut out the items and place them in the appropriate rooms in Blackline Master 7a. Model any words students want to know. Ask volunteers to show their pictures to the class and name items they have chosen.

Identify kinds of housing

Identify furniture and rooms

Read for-rent signs

Ask about the rent and the deposit

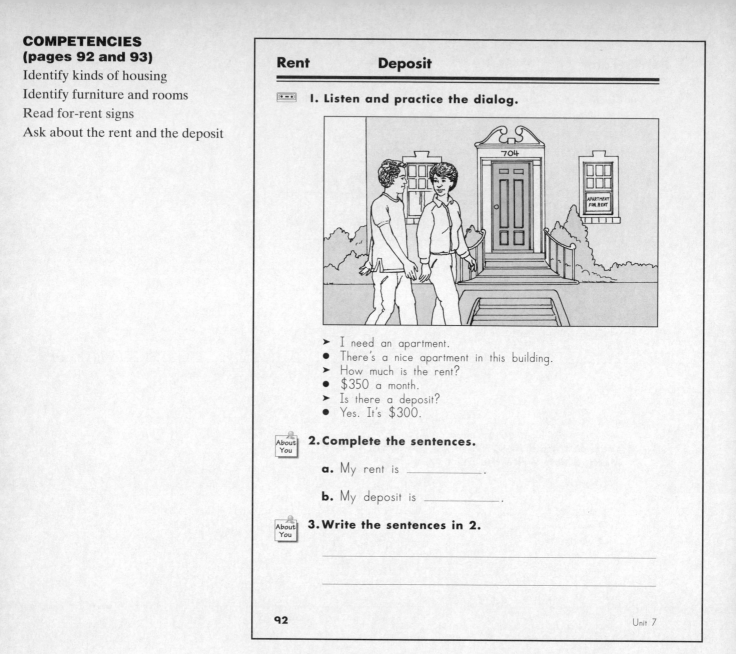

Rent   Deposit

I. Listen and practice the dialog.

➤ I need an apartment.
● There's a nice apartment in this building.
➤ How much is the rent?
● $350 a month.
➤ Is there a deposit?
● Yes. It's $300.

2. Complete the sentences.

a. My rent is _____.

b. My deposit is _____.

3. Write the sentences in 2.

_____

_____

92   Unit 7

PREPARATION

Preteach the new language in the lesson. Follow these suggestions.

● Use word cards, a picture of an apartment, play money or Blackline Master 5: Money, and a calendar to preteach the recognition words **rent** and **deposit.** To teach **rent,** point to each month in turn on the calendar and say, *The rent is $350 a month.* Hold up the word card for **rent** and display $350 in play money. To teach **deposit,** indicate the picture of the apartment and say, *I want this apartment.* Hold up the rent money as well as $300 more in play money. Indicate the rent money and say, *This is the rent.* Then indicate the $300 and say, *This is the deposit. If the apartment is O.K. when I leave,*

they will return the deposit. Display and read the word cards and have students repeat.

● Preteach the dialog. Use pictures or the illustrations in this unit to teach the word **building.** Refer to the illustration on this page and say, *There's a nice apartment in this building.* Show a picture of the interior of a nice apartment. Have students repeat.

PRESENTATION

1. Focus attention on the illustration. Have students say as much as they can about it. You may want to cue students by indicating items for them to name or by saying names of items and having students indicate them. Restate students' ideas in acceptable

English and write them on the board or overhead projector.

Present the dialog. See "Presenting Dialogs" on page vii.

2. Help students read the directions. Demonstrate by completing the items for your rent and deposit (or for any reasonable rent and deposit) on the board or overhead projector. Students may also use fictitious amounts. Have them complete the exercise independently. Check students' work.

3. Help students read the directions. Complete the first item on the board or overhead projector. Then have students work to help each other complete the exercise. Ask volunteers to complete the sentences on the board or overhead

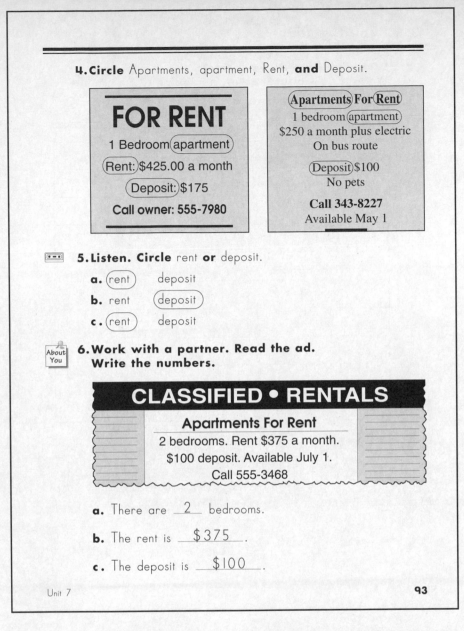

4. Circle Apartments, apartment, Rent, **and** Deposit.

FOR RENT

1 Bedroom apartment

Rent: $425.00 a month

Deposit: $175

Call owner: 555-7980

Apartments For Rent

1 bedroom apartment
$250 a month plus electric
On bus route

Deposit $100
No pets

Call 343-8227
Available May 1

5. Listen. Circle rent **or** deposit.

a. rent   deposit

b. rent   deposit

c. rent   deposit

**6. Work with a partner. Read the ad.
Write the numbers.**

CLASSIFIED • RENTALS

Apartments For Rent
2 bedrooms. Rent $375 a month.
$100 deposit. Available July 1.
Call 555-3468

a. There are __2__ bedrooms.

b. The rent is __$375__.

c. The deposit is __$100__.

---

projector. Check students' work.

4. Help students read the directions. Demonstrate by completing the first item on the board or overhead projector. Then have students complete the exercise in pairs. Ask volunteers to circle the answers on the board or overhead projector. Check students' work.

5. Help students read the directions. Then present the listening. See "Presenting Listenings" on page vii. Ask volunteers to read the answers aloud.

6. Help students read the directions. Have them say as much as they can about the ad. Then complete the first item on the board or overhead projector. Have students work in pairs to complete the exer-

cise. Ask volunteers to read the answers aloud and write them on the board or overhead projector. Then check students' work.

FOLLOW-UP

Selecting an Apartment: Provide pairs of students with classified ads for apartments for rent. Ask students to choose apartments they would like to rent and tell their partners the rent and, if stated, the deposit. Ask volunteers to tell the class about the apartments they chose: how many rooms they have, how much the rent is, and, if possible, what the deposit is. Have students use Blackline Master 6: Blank Check to write rent checks or deposit checks, or both.

♦ Review the dialog on page 92. Ask

pairs of students to use the dialog as a model and have conversations about the apartments they selected. Circulate to assist as needed. Ask several pairs to repeat their conversations for the class.

What furniture do you have?
Write the furniture under the room.

| bed | sofa | chair | lamp | refrigerator | stove | table |

Living Room	Bedroom	Bathroom	Kitchen
	bed		

PREPARATION

On the board or overhead projector, write the words **bed, sofa, chair, table, lamp, refrigerator, stove, living room, bedroom, bathroom,** and **kitchen.** Ask volunteers to read the words aloud and find the matching picture card for each.

PRESENTATION

Help students read the directions. Copy the chart on the board or overhead projector. Demonstrate by filling in the furniture in your living room. Then have students work in pairs to help each other complete the activity. Erase your information and ask several volunteers in turn to fill it in with their answers. Check students' work.

FOLLOW-UP

Rooms and Furniture: Provide each pair of students with a copy of Blackline Master 7a: Rooms and Blackline Master 7b: Furniture. Have students cut out the furniture and take turns telling each other which room to put each item of furniture in. Circulate to assist as needed. Have students change partners and repeat the activity. Ask several pairs to repeat their conversations for the class.

◆ Have students count off by twos. Distribute copies of the blackline masters to the "ones." Have them make an inappropriate furniture arrangement by placing items of furniture on the blackline master rooms. (For example, they can put a

stove in the bedroom, an upholstered chair in the bathroom, etc.) Caution them not to show the arrangement to their partners. Then have the "twos" instruct the "ones" as necessary to fix the arrangements. Have them switch roles and repeat the activity.

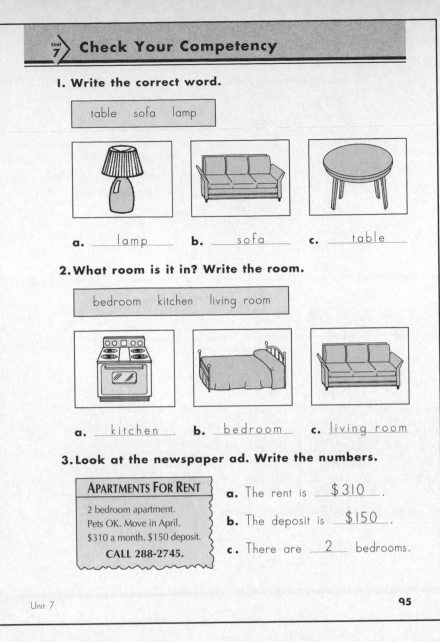

1. Write the correct word.

table sofa lamp

a. __lamp__   b. __sofa__   c. __table__

2. What room is it in? Write the room.

bedroom kitchen living room

a. __kitchen__   b. __bedroom__   c. __living room__

3. Look at the newspaper ad. Write the numbers.

APARTMENTS FOR RENT

2 bedroom apartment.
Pets OK. Move in April.
$310 a month. $150 deposit.
CALL 288-2745.

a. The rent is __$310__.

b. The deposit is __$150__.

c. There are __2__ bedrooms.

Unit 7   **95**

PREPARATION

Briefly review the new language in this unit before students open their books. Write the words on the board or overhead projector and ask volunteers to find matching picture cards for each.

Write **table, sofa, lamp, bedroom, kitchen,** and **living room** on the board or overhead projector. Read the words with the class. Ask students to name furniture they would put in each room and find matching picture cards.

Ask students to say how much they think the rent and deposit for a two-bedroom apartment would be. Write the responses on the board or overhead projector.

Provide specific help as needed until you are sure students feel confident that they know all the new language.

PRESENTATION

Use any of the procedures in "Evaluation," page viii, with these pages. Record individuals' results on the Unit 7 Individual Competency Chart. Record the class's results on the Class Cumulative Competency Chart.

FOLLOW-UP

An Optional Cooperative Learning Activity: Set up "Apartment Rental Agencies" at several locations around the room. Pin or tape ads for apartments to the wall behind each

location. Ask volunteers to serve as rental agents. Have the rest of the students, in pairs, imagine that they are people looking for apartments. Ask the renters to decide what kinds of apartments they are looking for (how many bedrooms and bathrooms they want, whether they want the apartment furnished or unfurnished, and the approximate rent they want to pay). Then have renters each visit one of the rental agencies and describe the apartments they want. If the agent doesn't have an apartment the renters like, the renters can visit different agencies. Circulate to assist as needed.

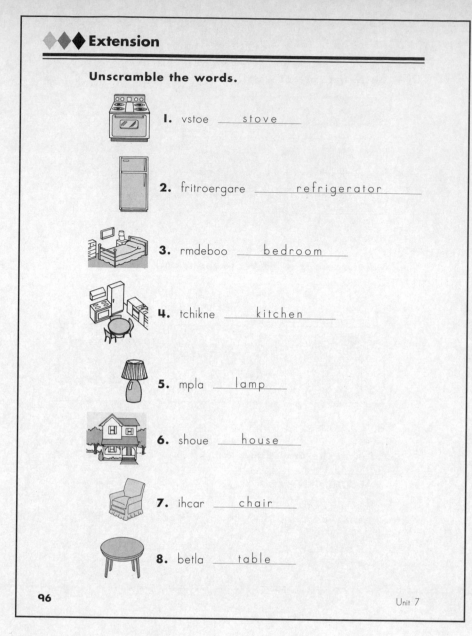

Unscramble the words.

1. vstoe _____stove_____

2. fritroergare _____refrigerator_____

3. rmdeboo _____bedroom_____

4. tchikne _____kitchen_____

5. mpla _____lamp_____

6. shoue _____house_____

7. ihcar _____chair_____

8. betla _____table_____

96   Unit 7

PREPARATION

Brainstorm with the students all the names of furniture and rooms they learned in this unit. Write them on the board or overhead projector and read them aloud. Ask volunteers to illustrate the meaning of the words by referring to the blackline masters, picture cards, and/or pictures in the book.

PRESENTATION

On each of five index cards, write one letter of the word **stove.** Shuffle the cards and place them side by side on the chalk rail next to the picture of the stove. Ask a volunteer to unscramble the word.

Have students identify the pictures.

Then have them work in pairs to complete the activity. When students complete the activity, ask volunteers to say the words aloud and write them on the board or overhead projector.

Health Care

Look at the picture.

Where are the people?

What are they doing?

97

1. Identify parts of the body
2. Describe symptoms and injuries
3. Read medicine labels
4. Make doctors' appointments

Unit 8 Optional Materials

● Picture cards and word cards for illnesses **(sore throat, fever, cough, headache, stomachache, cold, flu)** and kinds of medicine **(tablet, capsule).**

● Word cards for **arm, hand, foot, leg, sick, medicine, teaspoon,** and **tablespoon.**

● Realia: A variety of medicines, including tablets and capsules; a real or simulated doctor's prescription; a set of measuring spoons.

● Blackline Master 8: Human Body, page 150.

COMPETENCIES (page 97)

Identify parts of the body

Describe symptoms and injuries

PRESENTATION

Teaching Note: Use this page to warm up students, to check and draw on their prior knowledge, and to spark interest.

Read the unit title and questions aloud. Help students identify the situation. Encourage them to identify as many items in the picture as they can and to describe what is happening. As students may be able to say very little, you might have to prompt them by indicating items for them to name or by saying names of items

and having students indicate them. Repeat students' ideas or restate them in acceptable English. Model any words students do not know.

FOLLOW-UP

Community Health Services: Ask students to name places in the community they or other people go for help when they are sick. List on the board or overhead projector the places students name and add important clinics or hospitals they may have omitted. Ask students if they have ever gone to one of these places. Have volunteers share their experiences with the class.

◆ Have students watch as you look up the telephone numbers of the health facilities on the list in a tele-

phone directory. Write the numbers on the board or overhead projector. Give students time to copy the information they need.

Identify parts of the body

Describe symptoms and injuries

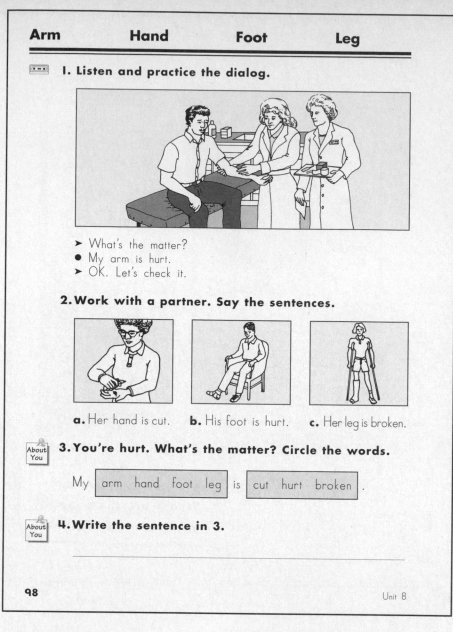

| Arm | Hand | Foot | Leg |

1. Listen and practice the dialog.

➤ What's the matter?
● My arm is hurt.
➤ OK. Let's check it.

2. Work with a partner. Say the sentences.

a. Her hand is cut. **b.** His foot is hurt. **c.** Her leg is broken.

About You **3. You're hurt. What's the matter? Circle the words.**

My | arm hand foot leg | is | cut hurt broken | .

About You **4. Write the sentence in 3.**

_____

98   Unit 8

PREPARATION

Preteach the new language in the lesson. Follow these suggestions.

● Use pantomime and/or Blackline Master 8: Human Body to preteach the recognition words **arm, hand, foot** and **leg**. See "Presenting Recognition Words" on page vii.

● Use pictures and pantomime to teach the words **hurt, cut,** and **broken.** Say each word and have students repeat.

● Preteach the dialog. Pretend to bump your arm. Grimace and say, _My arm is hurt._ Have students repeat. Then ask a volunteer to pretend to hurt his or her arm. Ask, _What's the matter?_ Prompt the student to answer, _My arm is hurt._ Say,

OK. Let's check it. Pretend to examine the student's arm.

PRESENTATION

1. Focus attention on the illustration. Have students say as much as they can about the illustration. You may want to cue them by indicating items for them to name or by saying names of items and having students indicate them. Restate students' ideas in acceptable English and write them on the board or overhead projector. Present the dialog. See "Presenting Dialogs" on page vii.

Teaching Note: You can use Blackline Master 8: Human Body to present additional parts of the body. Use the labeled picture to introduce

the new words. Then students can use the unlabeled picture to review the new words.

2. Have students read the directions and describe the illustration. Demonstrate the first item by saying the sentence with a volunteer. Then have students complete the exercise. Ask volunteers to say their sentences to the class.

About You **3.** Help students read the directions. If necessary, prompt the students by displaying a picture of someone with one of the symptoms in the sentence. (Or indicate one of the pictures in item 2.) Then have students complete the exercise. Ask a volunteer to read the answer aloud. Check students' work.

5. Write the words.

a. arm   b. leg   c. hand   d. foot

_____ _____ _____ _____

_____ _____ _____ _____

_____ _____ _____ _____

_____ _____ _____ _____

6. Listen. Circle the word you hear.

a. (arm)   leg

b. (hand)   foot

c. arm   (foot)

7. What's the matter? Complete the dialog.

➤ What's the matter?

● _____

8. Work with a partner. Practice the dialog in 7.

---

4. Help students read the directions. Complete the exercise on the board or overhead projector. Then have students complete the exercise. Check students' work.

5. Help students read the directions. Demonstrate by completing the first item on the board or overhead projector. Then have students complete the exercise. Check students' work.

6. Help students read the directions. Then present the listening. See "Presenting Listenings" on page vii. Ask volunteers to read the correct answers aloud and indicate the body part on themselves or Blackline Master 8: Human Body.

7. Help students read the directions. With students,

brainstorm possible answers and write them on the board or overhead projector. Then demonstrate by writing an answer to the question on the board or overhead projector. Have students complete the exercise. Ask volunteers to read their answers aloud. Check students' work.

8. Help students read the directions. Demonstrate with a volunteer. Then have students complete the exercise. Have students change partners and repeat the exercise. Ask several pairs to say their conversations for the class.

FOLLOW-UP

Identifying Parts of the Body: Have students stand. Give a series of commands, such as **Touch your (foot).**

Demonstrate by giving the command and doing the action yourself. Then ask the class to perform the action as you say it.

♦ One at a time, hold up word cards with the names of parts of the body and ask each student to touch that part of his or her body.

Identify parts of the body

Describe symptoms and injuries

Make doctors' appointments

PREPARATION

Preteach the new language in the lesson. Follow these suggestions.

● Use picture cards, word cards, pantomime, and/or the illustrations in the book to preteach the recognition words **sick, sore throat, fever,** and **cough.** See "Presenting Recognition Words" on page vii.

● To review or preteach time and days of the week, follow the instructions on pages 50 and 52.

● Preteach the dialog. Use pictures or illustrations in this unit to teach or review the words **doctor** and **office.** Then discuss the picture at the top of this page. Identify the receptionist's location as Dr. Kendell's office, and have students repeat.

PRESENTATION

1. Focus attention on the illustration. Have students say as much as they can about it. You may want to cue them by indicating items for them to name or by saying names of items and having students indicate them. Restate students' ideas in acceptable English and write them on the board or overhead projector.

Present the dialog. See "Presenting Dialogs" on page vii.

2. Help students read the directions. Discuss the pictures. Demonstrate by saying the words with a volunteer. Then have students complete the exercise in pairs. Ask volunteers to say the words aloud to the class.

3. Help students read the directions. If necessary, prompt

the students by displaying a picture of someone with one of the symptoms in the sentence. (Or indicate one of the pictures in item 2.) Have students complete the exercise. Ask volunteers to read their answers aloud. Check students' work.

4. Help students read the directions. Demonstrate by writing the sentence on the board or overhead projector. Then have students complete the exercise. Ask a volunteer to read the sentence aloud. Check students' work.

5. Help students read the directions. Demonstrate by completing the first item on the board or overhead projector. Then have students complete the exercise. Check students' work.

6. Help students read the directions.

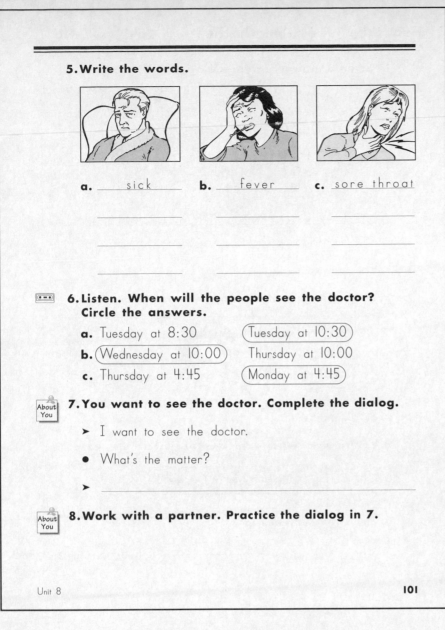

5. Write the words.

a. ___sick___

b. ___fever___

c. ___sore throat___

6. Listen. When will the people see the doctor? Circle the answers.

a. Tuesday at 8:30   (Tuesday at 10:30)

b. (Wednesday at 10:00)   Thursday at 10:00

c. Thursday at 4:45   (Monday at 4:45)

7. You want to see the doctor. Complete the dialog.

➤ I want to see the doctor.

● What's the matter?

➤ _____

8. Work with a partner. Practice the dialog in 7.

Then present the listening. See "Presenting Listenings" on page vii. Ask volunteers to read the correct answers aloud. You might also have them set the times on Blackline Master 4: Clock, page 145.

7. Help students read the directions. With students, brainstorm possible answers and write them on the board or overhead projector. Then have students complete the exercise. Ask volunteers to read their answers aloud. Check students' work.

8. Help students read the directions. Demonstrate by saying the dialog with a volunteer. Have students say the dialog in pairs, then switch roles and repeat. Ask several pairs to say their conversations for the class.

FOLLOW-UP

What's the Matter? Write the names of illnesses on separate index cards. Pantomime an illness and have students figure out the illness. When they answer correctly, show them the card. Then give a card to each of several volunteers. Have them take turns pantomiming the illnesses while the rest of the class tries to figure out what's the matter.

◆ Give each student an index card and have him or her write the name of an illness. Then have students in small groups take turns pantomiming their illnesses as the rest of the group tries to figure out what's the matter.

Identify parts of the body

Describe symptoms and injuries

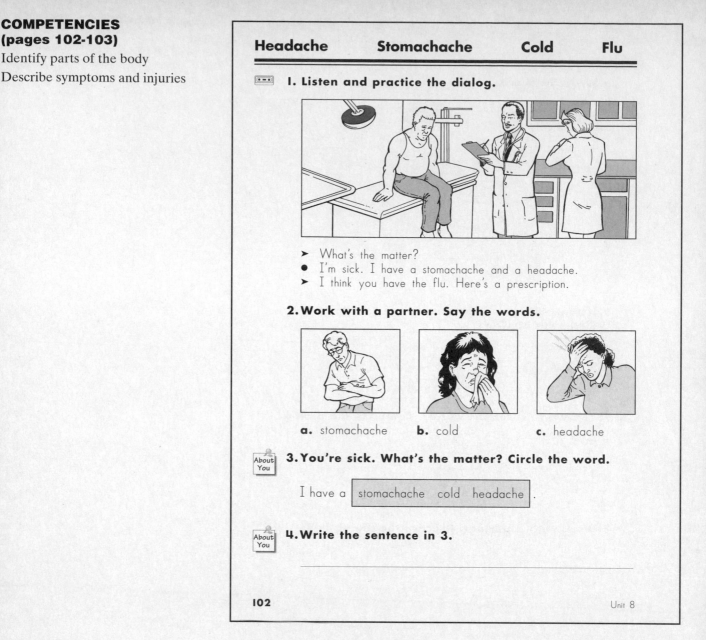

| Headache | Stomachache | Cold | Flu |

1. Listen and practice the dialog.

➤ What's the matter?
● I'm sick. I have a stomachache and a headache.
➤ I think you have the flu. Here's a prescription.

2. Work with a partner. Say the words.

a. stomachache   **b.** cold   **c.** headache

About You **3. You're sick. What's the matter? Circle the word.**

I have a [stomachache   cold   headache].

About You **4. Write the sentence in 3.**

102   Unit 8

PREPARATION

Preteach the new language in the lesson. Follow these suggestions.

● Use picture cards, pantomime, and word cards to preteach the recognition words **headache, stomachache, cold,** and **flu.** See "Presenting Recognition Words" on page vii.

● Preteach the dialog. To teach **prescription,** show a doctor's prescription or use the picture on the page. Explain that patients must see doctors to get prescriptions. Patients then go to the drug store to buy the medicine.

PRESENTATION

1. Focus attention on the illustration. Have students say as much as they can about it. You may want to cue them by indicating items for them to name or by saying names of items and having students indicate them. Restate students' ideas in acceptable English and write them on the board or overhead projector.

Present the dialog. See "Presenting Dialogs" on page vii.

2. Help students read the directions. Discuss the pictures. Demonstrate by saying the words with a volunteer. Then have students complete the exercise in pairs. Ask volunteers to say the words to the class.

About You **3.** Help students read the directions. Display a picture of someone with one of the symptoms. Or indicate one of the pictures in item 2. Then have students complete the exercise. Ask a volunteer to read the answer aloud. Check students' work.

About You **4.** Help students read the directions. Demonstrate by writing the sentence on the board or overhead projector. Then have students complete the exercise. Ask a volunteer to read the sentence aloud. Check students' work.

5. Help students read the directions. Demonstrate by completing the first item on the board or overhead projector. Then have students complete the exercise. Ask volunteers to write the answers on the board or overhead projector. Check students' work.

6. Help students read the directions. Then present the listening. See

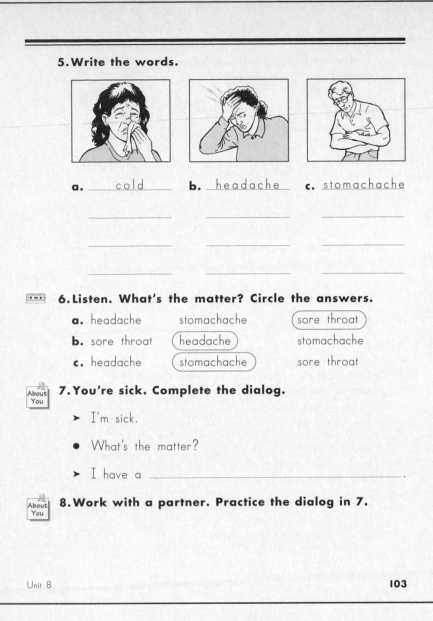

5. Write the words.

a. <u>cold</u> **b.** <u>headache</u> **c.** <u>stomachache</u>

_____ _____ _____

_____ _____ _____

_____ _____ _____

6. Listen. What's the matter? Circle the answers.

a. headache stomachache (sore throat)

b. sore throat (headache) stomachache

c. headache (stomachache) sore throat

7. You're sick. Complete the dialog.

➤ I'm sick.

● What's the matter?

➤ I have a _____.

8. Work with a partner. Practice the dialog in 7.

"Presenting Listenings" on page vii. Ask volunteers to read the correct answers aloud and to match them to picture cards or pictures in the book.

7. Help students read the directions. With students, brainstorm possible answers and write them on the board or overhead projector. Then have students complete the exercise. Ask volunteers to read their answers aloud. Check students' work.

8. Help students read the directions. Demonstrate by saying the dialog with a volunteer. Have students say the dialog in pairs. Have students change partners and repeat. Ask several pairs to say their conversations for the class.

FOLLOW-UP

Common Illnesses: Provide each pair of students with a copy of Blackline Master 8: Human Body. On the board or overhead projector, write the words **headache, stomachache, cold, flu, cough,** and **sore throat.** Ask pairs to take turns naming these illnesses and pointing to the places on the body that each one affects.

♦ Ask pairs of students to write the names of the illnesses on the copies of the blackline master next to the parts of the body they affect. Explain that they can write an illness in more than one place. Sketch the body on the board or overhead projector and have volunteers write their answers in the appropriate spots. Check students' work.

Describe symptoms and injuries
Read medicine labels

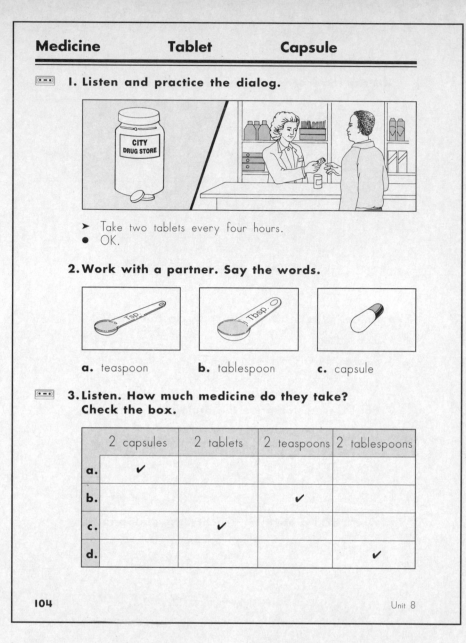

Medicine   Tablet   Capsule

1. Listen and practice the dialog.

➤ Take two tablets every four hours.
● OK.

2. Work with a partner. Say the words.

a. teaspoon   **b.** tablespoon   **c.** capsule

**3. Listen. How much medicine do they take?
Check the box.**

	2 capsules	2 tablets	2 teaspoons	2 tablespoons
a.	✔			
b.			✔	
c.		✔		
d.				✔

104   Unit 8

PREPARATION

Preteach the new language in the lesson. Follow these suggestions.

● To teach the concept of medicine, pantomime feeling ill by coughing, blowing your nose, putting your hand to your head, etc. Then pantomime taking medicine and feeling better. Finally, show a number of different medicines and say of each, *This is medicine.*

● Use picture cards, realia items, and word cards to preteach the recognition words **medicine, tablet, capsule, teaspoon,** and **tablespoon.** See "Presenting Recognition Words" on page vii.

● Preteach the dialog. Display two tablets and say, *Take two tablets every four hours.* Have students

repeat. To demonstrate **every four hours,** work out a time schedule on the board or overhead projector. (For example: 6 A.M., 10 A.M., 2 P.M., 6 P.M., 10 P.M., and 2 A.M.) Use Blackline Master 4: Clock to count out the hours for students.

PRESENTATION

1. Focus attention on the illustration. Help students identify the place and the people. Have students say as much as they can about the illustration. You may want to cue them by indicating items for them to name or by saying names of items and having students indicate them. Restate students' ideas in acceptable English and write them on the board or overhead projector.

Present the dialog. See "Presenting Dialogs" on page vii.

2. Help students read the directions. Discuss the pictures. Demonstrate by saying the words with a volunteer. Then have students complete the exercise in pairs. Ask volunteers to say the words aloud to the class.

3. Help students read the directions. Then present the listening. See "Presenting Listenings" on page vii. Ask volunteers to check the correct boxes on the board or overhead projector and read the answers aloud. Check students' work.

4. Help students read the directions. Demonstrate by completing the first item on the board or overhead projector. Then have students complete the exercise. Check students' work.

4. Match.

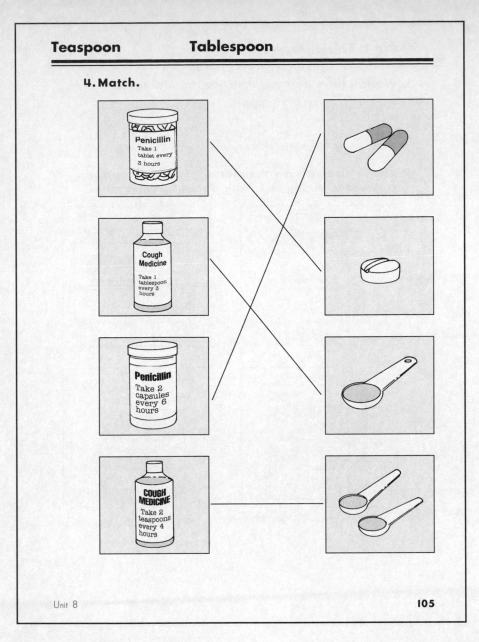

FOLLOW-UP

Following the Directions: Have available a number of "capsules" and "tablets", a bottle of liquid, and a set of measuring spoons. In advance, prepare a variety of "prescriptions" on index cards. Have students come forward, one at a time, choose a card at random, read it to the class, and measure out the appropriate amount of "medicine." Ask each student, *If you take the medicine now, what time will you take it again?*

♦ Repeat the activity, but this time have each student write a direction line he or she might find on a prescription. Arrange students in pairs and have them exchange "prescriptions," then come forward, one at a time, to demonstrate following the directions.

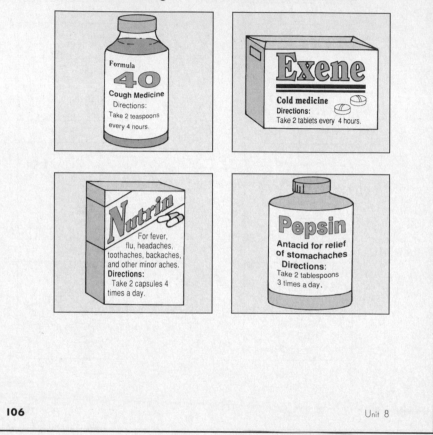

◆ Put It Together

1. Work with a partner. Practice the dialog.

> ➤ I'm sick. I have a headache.
> ● Take Nutrin.
> ➤ How much?
> ● Take two capsules, four times a day.

2. You're sick. What's the matter? Tell your partner. Follow the dialog in 1. Talk about the medicine.

PREPARATION

On the board or overhead projector, write the words **sick, headache, capsules, cough, medicine, teaspoon, tablespoon, tablets, fever, flu,** and **stomachache.** Ask volunteers to read the words aloud and find a matching picture card or picture in the book for each.

PRESENTATION

1. Help students read the directions. Model the dialog with a volunteer. Have students say the dialog in pairs. Have them switch roles and say the dialog again. Have several pairs say their conversations for the class.

2. Help students read the directions. Discuss the illustrations and model any words students want to know.

Then model a conversation about the first item with a volunteer. Have students complete the activity. Ask students to change partners and repeat the activity. Have several pairs say their conversations for the class.

FOLLOW-UP

More About Medicine: Bring in (or have students bring in) the packaging from real medicines. Try to have one package per student. Distribute the packages and have each student tell the class about the medicine. Have them say what the medicine is for, how much should be taken, and how often it should be taken. Model any words students want to know.

◆ Duplicate copies of newspaper advertisements or flyers from drug

stores. Arrange students in small groups and distribute a set to each. Have them circle all the medicines they see in the flyers and talk about what the medicines are for. Circulate to assist as needed. Model any words students want to know. Ask a volunteer from each group to name and describe one medicine they see in the flyers.

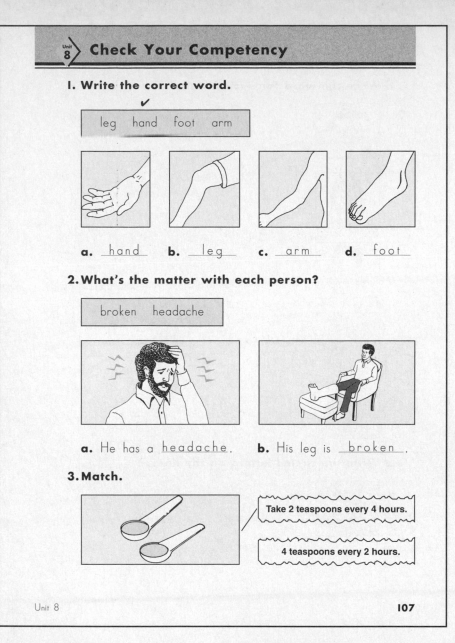

1. Write the correct word.

leg hand foot arm

a. hand **b.** leg **c.** arm **d.** foot

2. What's the matter with each person?

broken headache

a. He has a headache. **b.** His leg is broken.

3. Match.

Take 2 teaspoons every 4 hours.

4 teaspoons every 2 hours.

Unit 8   **107**

PREPARATION

Briefly review the new language in this unit before students open their books. Write the words on the board or overhead projector. Ask volunteers to find the matching picture cards or indicate appropriate pictures in their books.

On the board or overhead projector, write **Take three teaspoons every two hours** and **Take two teaspoons every three hours.** Read these sentences aloud. Draw two spoons on the board near the instructions. Ask a volunteer to draw a line matching the spoons with the appropriate sentence.

Provide specific help as needed until you are sure students feel confident that they know all the new language.

PRESENTATION

Use any of the procedures in "Evaluation," page viii, with these pages. Record individuals' results on the Unit 8 Individual Competency Chart. Record the class's results on the Class Cumulative Competency Chart.

FOLLOW-UP

An Optional Cooperative Learning Activity: Add evidence of illnesses to Blackline Master 8: Human Body. For example, show cuts on the hand and foot, pain lines coming from the head and stomach, a splint on the leg, etc. Arrange students in small groups and distribute a copy of the altered blackline master to each. Ask students to take turns telling their

group something that is wrong with the person. Circulate to assist as needed. Ask volunteers to tell the class what is wrong with the person.

I. Write the word for each picture.

H E A (D) A C H E

C (O) L D

(C) O U G H

S O R E (T) H R (O) A T

F E V E (R)

2. Write the circled letters on the lines.

D O C T O R

108   Unit 8

PREPARATION

With students, brainstorm a list of words they've learned in this unit. Write them on the board or overhead projector and read them aloud. Ask volunteers to find corresponding picture cards or pictures in the book.

PRESENTATION

1. Help students read the directions. Demonstrate by completing the first item on the board or overhead projector. Then have students complete the activity. Have volunteers share their answers with the class.

2. Help students read the directions. Demonstrate by filling in the first letter on the board or overhead projector. Have students complete the rest of the activity in pairs. Circulate to

assist as needed. Ask a volunteer to share the answers with the class.

Employment

MIDNIGHT Diner

HELP WANTED COOK

Look at the picture.

Where are the people?

What are they doing?

109

Unit 9 Overview

UNIT COMPETENCIES

1. Identify kinds of jobs
2. Give your work experience
3. Give and follow instructions
4. Read help-wanted signs
5. Complete a simple job application

Unit 9 Optional Materials

● Word cards and picture cards for **days** and **nights.**

● Word cards for **job, application, experience, weekends, help wanted,** and **pay.**

● Pictures of types of jobs in the unit (painter, custodian, cook, clerk, mechanic, housekeeper).

● Realia: A calendar; the help-wanted section of a newspaper.

♦ Blackline Master 9: Job Application, page 151.

COMPETENCIES (page 109)

Identify kinds of jobs

PRESENTATION

Teaching Note: Use this page to warm up students, to check and draw on their prior knowledge, and to spark interest.

Read the unit title and questions aloud. Encourage students to identify the people and the place and to describe what is happening. As students may be able to say very little, you might have to prompt them by indicating items for them to name or by saying names of items and having students indicate them. Repeat students' ideas or restate them in acceptable English. Model any words

students do not know.

FOLLOW-UP

Jobs In a Restaurant: Point out the help-wanted sign in the picture. Help students read **Cook.** If necessary, use pantomime to clarify the meaning of **cook.** With students, brainstorm a list of other jobs in a restaurant. Encourage students to pantomime the jobs if they don't know the words for them. Write the words on the board or overhead projector and read them aloud.

♦ Brainstorm other jobs that might be available in your community and add them to the list. If students have applied for jobs, encourage them to share their experiences with the class.

Job

🔲 **I. Listen and practice the dialog.**

➤ I want a job.
● What do you do?
➤ I'm a cook.

2. Work with a partner. Say the names of the jobs.

a. painter   **b.** custodian   **c.** cook

d. clerk   **e.** mechanic   **f.** housekeeper

🔲 **3. Listen. Circle the job you hear.**

a. custodian   (cook)

b. painter   (clerk)

c. (mechanic)   housekeeper

110   Unit 9

PREPARATION

Preteach the new language in the lesson. Follow these suggestions.

● To teach the word **job,** say *I have a job. I'm a teacher.* Ask volunteers to tell you what their jobs are. See "Presenting Recognition Words" on page vii.

● Use pictures or the illustrations in the book to preteach the words **painter, custodian, cook, clerk, mechanic,** and **housekeeper.**

● Preteach the dialog. To teach the question *What do (you) do?,* hold up pictures of people working. For each person, ask, *What does (he) do?* Have students repeat. Then model the answer.

PRESENTATION

1. Focus attention on the illustration. Have students say as much as they can about it. You may want to cue them by indicating items for them to name or by saying names of items and having students indicate them. Restate students' ideas in acceptable English and write them on the board or overhead projector.

Present the dialog. See "Presenting Dialogs" on page vii.

2. Help students read the directions. Discuss the pictures. Demonstrate by saying the jobs with a volunteer. Then have students complete the exercise in pairs. Ask volunteers to say the names aloud to the class.

3. Help students read the directions. Then present the listening. See

"Presenting Listenings" on page vii. Ask volunteers to read the correct answers aloud and indicate a corresponding picture for each.

4. Help students read the directions. Encourage them to say as much as they can about the illustration. Demonstrate by completing the first item on the board or overhead projector. Have students complete the exercise. Ask volunteers to circle correct answers on the board or overhead projector. Check students' work.

5. Help students read the directions. Demonstrate by completing the first item on the board or overhead projector. Then have students complete the exercise independently. Check students' work.

4. Circle PAINTER, CUSTODIAN, HOUSEKEEPER, **and** MECHANIC.

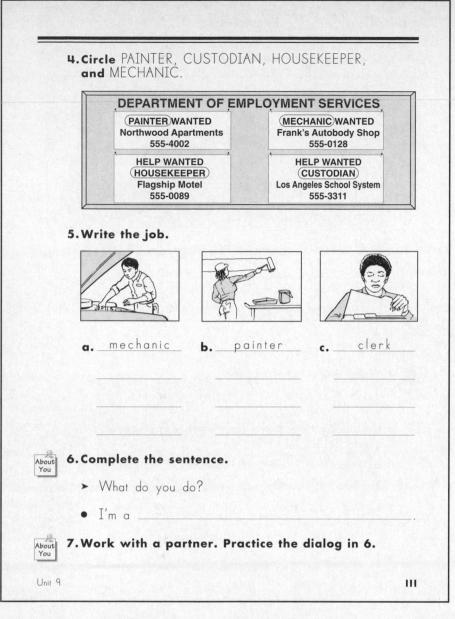

DEPARTMENT OF EMPLOYMENT SERVICES

(PAINTER) WANTED
Northwood Apartments
555-4002

(MECHANIC) WANTED
Frank's Autobody Shop
555-0128

HELP WANTED
(HOUSEKEEPER)
Flagship Motel
555-0089

HELP WANTED
(CUSTODIAN)
Los Angeles School System
555-3311

5. Write the job.

a. mechanic

b. painter

c. clerk

6. Complete the sentence.

➤ What do you do?

● I'm a _____.

7. Work with a partner. Practice the dialog in 6.

Unit 9   III

---

6. Help students read the directions. Brainstorm with students possible choices for the answer. Write them on the board or overhead projector. Complete the sentence using yourself as an example. Have students complete the exercise in pairs. Then ask volunteers to read their answers aloud. Check students' work.

7. Help students read the directions. Demonstrate with a volunteer. Take turns beginning the conversation. Then have students complete the exercise in pairs. Have students change partners and repeat the exercise. Ask several pairs to say their conversations for the class.

Teaching Note: You might present the names of jobs available to students in your community or jobs that students actually have.

FOLLOW-UP

What Do You Do? Write the names of jobs on separate index cards. Pantomime a job and encourage students to figure out what it is. When they answer correctly show them the card. Then give a card to each of several volunteers. Have them take turns pantomiming the jobs while the rest of the class tries to figure them out.

♦ Provide index cards and have each student write the name of a job. Then have students in small groups take turns pantomiming their jobs as the rest of the group tries to figure out the jobs.

COMPETENCIES
(pages 112-113)

Give your work experience

Give and follow instructions

Read help-wanted signs

Complete a simple job application

Application   Experience

🔲 **1. Listen and practice the dialog.**

➤ I want to apply for the job.
● Do you have any experience?
➤ Yes, I do. I was a cook from 1991 to 1993.
● OK. Please complete this application.

2. Complete the sentence.

I was a _____ from _____ to _____.

3. Write the sentence in 2.

_____

🔲 **4. Listen. Do they have any work experience?**
Circle Yes **or** No.

a. Ignacio   (Yes)   No

b. Anna   Yes   (No)

c. May   (Yes)   No

112   Unit 9

PREPARATION

Preteach the new language in the lesson. Follow these suggestions.

● To teach the word **experience,** list a few jobs on the board with time periods for each. Show a picture of a person. For each job on the list say, *From (1991 to 1992) (she) was a (job title).* Indicate the entire list, and say, *This is (her) experience.* Write **experience** above the list.

● Use a word card and Blackline Master 9: Job Application to preteach the recognition word **application.** See "Presenting Recognition Words" on page vii.

● Preteach the dialog. To teach **apply,** show students a real application (or Blackline Master 9) and say, *I want to apply for a job. I have to*

complete an application. Have students repeat.

PRESENTATION

1. Focus attention on the illustration. Have students say as much as they can about it. You may want to cue them by indicating items for them to name or by saying names of items and having students indicate them. Restate students' ideas in acceptable English and write them on the board or overhead projector.

Present the dialog. See "Presenting Dialogs" on page vii.

2. Help students read the directions. Demonstrate on the board or overhead projector by completing the item with personal (or fictitious) information. Brainstorm with

students possible job choices for the answer. Then have students work in pairs to complete the sentence. Ask volunteers to read their sentences aloud. Check students' work.

3. Help students read the directions. Demonstrate by copying your sentence on the board. Then have students complete the exercise. Ask volunteers to write their sentences on the board or overhead projector. Check students' work.

4. Help students read the directions. Then present the listening. See "Presenting Listenings" on page vii. Ask volunteers to read the correct answers aloud.

5. Help students read the directions. Demonstrate by completing the first

5. Circle Experience **and** Application.

Job (Application)			
Name: Li Chiu			Telephone Number: (712) 555-6321
Address: 3701 Hart Lane, Apt. 21 Sacramento, CA 97521			
Work (Experience)			
From	To	Job	Employer
1990	1993	Housekeeper	Memorial Hospital
1986	1990	Clerk	Chan Exports

6. Look at the application in 5. Answer the questions.

a. When was Li Chiu a housekeeper?

_____ From 1990 to 1993 _____

b. Where was she a housekeeper?

_____ Memorial Hospital _____

[About You] **7. Complete the application.**

Job Application			
Name:			Telephone Number:
Address:			
Work Experience			
From	To	Job	Employer

---

item on the board or overhead projector. Have students complete the exercise. Ask volunteers to circle the correct answers on the board or overhead projector. Check students' work.

6. Help students read the directions. Ask volunteers to read the questions aloud. Demonstrate by completing the first item on the board or overhead projector. Then have students answer the questions. Ask volunteers to write answers on the board or overhead projector. Check students' work.

[About You] **7.** Help students read the directions. Demonstrate by completing a sample application on the board or overhead projector. Then have students complete the

activity. Check students' work.

FOLLOW-UP

Job Experience: Tell students your job experience. Write the jobs and the time periods on the board or overhead projector. Then arrange students in pairs to tell each other about their job experience. Circulate to assist as needed. Model any words students want to know. Have them change partners and repeat the activity. Ask volunteers to repeat their conversations for the class.

♦ Brainstorm with students a list of businesses or companies in your community where students' friends or relatives work. Ask students if they know if these companies have entry-level jobs available.

Give and follow instructions

Complete a simple job application

Days   Nights   Weekends

🔲 **I. Listen and practice the dialog.**

➤ Can you work nights?
• Yes, I can.
➤ Can you work weekends?
• No, I can't. I'm sorry.
➤ When can you start?
• Immediately.
➤ OK. Be here tomorrow night at 5:00.

📝 **2. Complete the sentences.**
Write days, nights, **and** weekends.

I can work _____ .

I can't work _____ .

📝 **3. Write the sentences in 2.**

_____

_____

114   Unit 9

PREPARATION

Preteach the new language in the lesson. Follow these suggestions.

● Use word cards, picture cards, and a calendar to preteach the recognition words **days, nights,** and **weekends.** See "Presenting Recognition Words" on page vii.

● Preteach the dialog. To teach **can** and **can't,** ask a student, *Can you speak (student's native language)?* Help the student answer, *Yes, I can.* Then ask, *Can you speak (a language the student does not speak)?* Help the student answer, *No, I can't.* Then hold up the picture cards for **days** and **nights.** Indicate each in turn, and say, *I can work days. I can't work nights.* Have students repeat.

To teach **immediately,** tell students

you are going to open the door *immediately.* Then carry out the action very quickly. Ask students to perform actions such as standing up or opening their books immediately.

PRESENTATION

1. Focus attention on the illustration. Have students say as much as they can about it. You may want to cue them by indicating items for them to name or by saying names of items and having students indicate them. Restate students' ideas in acceptable English and write them on the board or overhead projector.

Present the dialog. See "Presenting Dialogs" on page vii.

📝 **2.** Help students read the directions. Demonstrate on the

board or overhead projector by completing the first item with personal (or fictitious) information. Then have students complete the sentences. Ask volunteers to read their sentences aloud. Check students' work.

📝 **3.** Help students read the directions. Demonstrate by copying your sentences on the board or overhead projector. Then have students complete the exercise. Ask volunteers to write their sentences on the board. Check students' work.

4. Help students read the directions. Demonstrate by circling the first item on the board or overhead projector. Have students complete the exercise. Check students' work.

5. Help students read the directions.

4. Circle days, nights, **and** weekends.

Name: *Tom Fitzgerald*   Telephone Number: *(534) 555-3678*
Address: *615 Western Ave. San Francisco, CA 92342*

AVAILABILITY

Can you work (weekends)?	(Yes)	No
Can you work (days)?	(Yes)	No
Can you work (nights)?	(Yes)	No

When can you start work?
Immediately   (In two weeks)   Other date: _____

5. Look at the application in 4. Circle the answers.

a. Can Tom work days?   (Yes)   No

b. Can Tom work weekends?   (Yes)   No

c. Can Tom work nights?   (Yes)   No

d. When can he start?   Immediately   (In two weeks)

About You **6. Complete the form.**

AVAILABILITY

Can you work weekends?	Yes	No
Can you work days?	Yes	No
Can you work nights?	Yes	No

When can you start work?
Immediately   In two weeks   Other date: _____

Ask volunteers to read the questions aloud. Demonstrate by completing the first item on the board or overhead projector. Then have students answer the questions. Ask volunteers to say their answers aloud and indicate an appropriate picture card or days on the calendar. Check students' work.

About You **6.** Help students read the directions. Complete a sample form on the board or overhead projector. Then have students complete the form. Ask volunteers to read their answers aloud and indicate appropriate picture cards or days on the calendar. Check students' work.

FOLLOW-UP

When Can You Work? Ask a volun-

teer questions about when he or she can work. Model the dialog on page 114. Then arrange students in pairs to have similar conversations. Have them take turns asking and answering the questions. Circulate to assist as needed. Have students change partners and repeat the activity. Ask several pairs to repeat their conversations for the class.

♦ Do a survey of your class to find out how many students can work days, nights, and/or weekends. Write the numbers on the board under the appropriate headings. Then have volunteers name jobs people might do in each of these time periods. List them under the appropriate headings.

Identify kinds of jobs

Give and follow instructions

Read help-wanted signs

Complete a simple job application

Help Wanted   Pay

I. Read the ads.

a.

HELP WANTED

Custodian—Monroe
Electronics Company
needs custodian

Experience required
$6.00 an hour

Apply in person
8868 Mountain Road

b.

**HELP
WANTED**

Painter wanted

No experience
necessary

Pay: $7.50 an hour

Call Tim's Painting

555-0012

2. Answer the questions. Write the letter of the ad.

a. The ad is for a custodian.   Ad __a__

b. No experience is required for this job.   Ad __b__

c. The pay is $6.00 an hour for this job.   Ad __a__

d. The ad is for a painter.   Ad __b__

e. Experience is required for this job.   Ad __a__

f. The pay is $7.50 an hour for this job.   Ad __b__

About You **3. Write. Which job do you want?**

Job applied for: _____

116   Unit 9

PREPARATION

Preteach the new language in the lesson. Follow these suggestions.

● Use word cards, the help-wanted section of a newspaper, and/or the illustrations in the book to preteach the recognition words **help wanted** and **pay.** See "Presenting Recognition Words" on page vii.

● Teach **Experience required** by writing **Help Wanted. Experience required.** on the board. Show two completed application forms, the first with nothing written in the experience section and the second with items written in. Hold up the first form, indicate the blank experience section, and say, *This person can't get this job.* Then show the second form, read the jobs listed in the experience

section, and say, *This person can get this job.* Then write **Help Wanted. No experience required.** Ask whether the people can get the job.

PRESENTATION

1. Focus attention on the help-wanted advertisements. Have students say as much as they can about them. Model the new language.

2. Help students read the directions. Demonstrate by completing the first item on the board or overhead projector. Have students complete the exercise. Ask volunteers to read the statements and tell which ad each refers to. Correct students' work.

About You **3.** Help students read the directions. Complete the exercise for yourself or for a volunteer.

Brainstorm with the class job choices other than those listed in the ads. Write them on the board or overhead projector. Then have students complete the exercise. Ask volunteers to read their answers to the class. Check students' work.

4. Help students read the directions. Demonstrate by completing the first item on the board or overhead projector. Then have students complete the exercise. Have volunteers circle the correct answers on the board or overhead projector. Check students' work.

About You **5.** Help students read the directions. Demonstrate by completing the application on the board or overhead projector. Ask several volunteers to read their

---

116   Real-Life English

4. Circle Help Wanted, experience, **and** Experience.

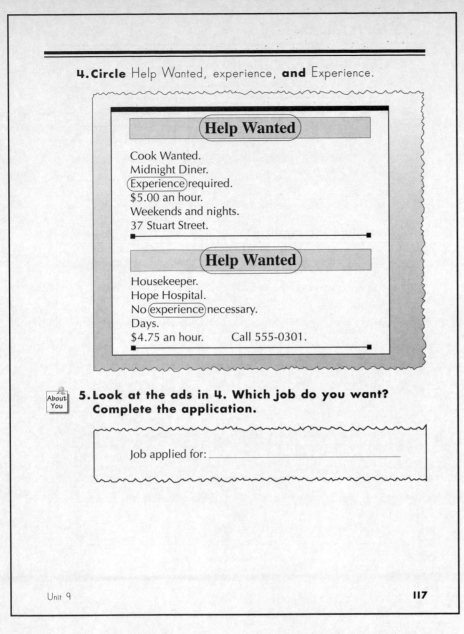

Help Wanted

Cook Wanted.
Midnight Diner.
(Experience) required.
$5.00 an hour.
Weekends and nights.
37 Stuart Street.

Help Wanted

Housekeeper.
Hope Hospital.
No (experience) necessary.
Days.
$4.75 an hour.   Call 555-0301.

About You

5. Look at the ads in 4. Which job do you want? Complete the application.

Job applied for: _____

answers to the class. Check students' work.

FOLLOW-UP

Filling Out Job Applications: Bring in sections of help-wanted ads from your community's newspaper that include jobs your students might be interested in. (You might enlarge them on a photocopier so students can read them easily.) Have each student find a job he or she might like to apply for. Ask students to work in pairs to help each other fill out applications for the jobs. Use Blackline Master 9: Job Application. Circulate to assist as needed and to model any words students want to know. Check students' work.

♦ Arrange students in small groups.

Have them take turns showing their group the help-wanted ads with the jobs they decided to apply for and reading their applications aloud.

◆ Put It Together

1. Look at the ads. Circle the job you want.

Mechanic needed—
Joe's Car Repair.
Full-time position.
$13.00 an hour.
Experience required.
Apply in person.
7 Unity Street.

Painter—
Dale's Painting Service.
Part-time position.
Experience preferred.
$9.00 an hour.
Call **555-2018.**

2. Complete the application.

JOB APPLICATION

Name: Telephone Number:

Address: Position Applied for:

WORK EXPERIENCE

From	To	Job	Employer

AVAILABILITY

Can you work days?	☐ Yes	☐ No
Can you work nights?	☐ Yes	☐ No
Can you work weekends?	☐ Yes	☐ No

When can you start work?

☐ Immediately   ☐ In two weeks

PREPARATION

On the board or overhead projector, write the words **mechanic** and **painter.** Ask volunteers to say the words aloud and find a matching picture card or illustration in the book for each type of job.

PRESENTATION

1. Help students read the directions. Demonstrate by telling students which job you want and circling it on the board or overhead projector. Then have students circle their choices.

2. Help students read the directions. Demonstrate by filling in the application on the board or overhead projector for the job you chose. Then have students fill in the application.

Circulate to assist as needed. Check students' work.

FOLLOW-UP

Job Interviews: To prepare students for job interviews, role-play a job interview with a volunteer as the rest of the class watches. When the interview is complete, ask the class to name the questions you asked. Write the questions on the board or overhead projector.

◆ Have the students use the list of questions to role-play job interviews of their own in pairs. Ask volunteers to repeat their interviews for the class.

I. Answer the questions. Circle the ad.

a.

Mechanic Wanted
Marty's Garage.
$12 an hour.
Experience Required.

b.

Cook Wanted
Ray's Hamburgers.
Pay: $5.50 an hour.
No experience required.

1. The ad is for a mechanic.   (Ad a)   Ad b
2. The job pays $5.50 an hour.   Ad a   (Ad b)
3. Experience is required for this job.   (Ad a)   Ad b

2. Complete the application.

JOB APPLICATION	
Name	Telephone Number
Address	
Position Applied for	

WORK EXPERIENCE			
From	To	Job	Employer

AVAILABILITY

	Yes	No
Can you work days?	☐	☐
Can you work nights?	☐	☐
Can you work weekends?	☐	☐

When can you start work?
☐ Immediately   ☐ In two weeks

PREPARATION

Briefly review the new language in this unit before students open their books. Write the words on the board or overhead projector and ask volunteers to find the matching picture cards or to indicate appropriate illustrations in their books.

Use the blackline master of a job application to help students review how to fill out a job application.

Provide specific help as needed until you are sure students feel confident that they know all the new words.

PRESENTATION

Use any of the procedures in "Evaluation," page viii, with these pages. Record individuals' results on the Unit 9 Individual Competency Chart. Record the class's results on the Class Cumulative Competency Chart.

FOLLOW-UP

An Optional Cooperative Learning Activity: Set up "employment agencies" at several places around the room. At each, display a variety of want ads that would be of interest to your students. Ask for volunteers to serve as "clerks" at the agencies. Ask the rest of the students to visit the agencies and ask questions about the jobs they see posted. Provide the clerks with copies of Blackline Master 9: Job Application. The clerk can hand an application to each student who visits the agency. Students can fill them out for the job they are interested in. Circulate to assist as needed. Check students' applications. As an extension of this activity, you might arrange for your class to visit a local employment office or for an interviewer to visit your classroom.

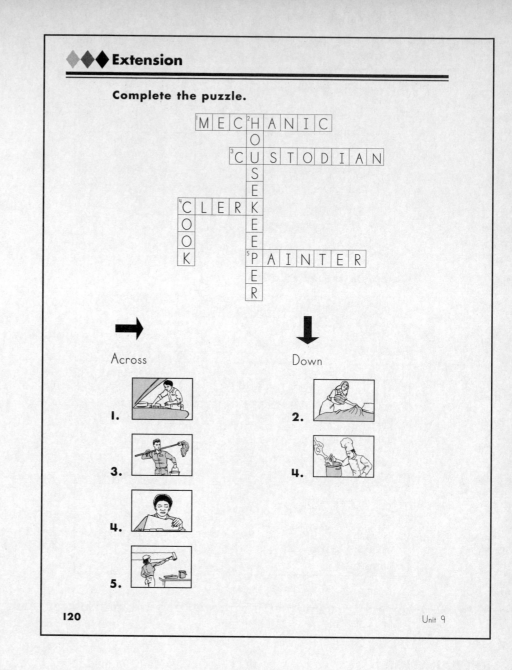

PREPARATION

With students, brainstorm a list of all the words they've learned in this unit. Write them on the board or overhead projector. Ask volunteers to find corresponding picture cards or illustrations in the book.

PRESENTATION

Help students read the directions. Point out and read the word **across.** Demonstrate by completing the first word across on the board or overhead projector. Emphasize that there is one letter per square. Repeat with **down.** Then have students complete the activity. Circulate to assist as needed. Correct the activity on the board or overhead projector. Check students' work.

Look at the picture.

Where are the people?

What are they doing?

121

Unit 10 Overview

UNIT COMPETENCIES

1. Identify kinds of transportation
2. Read traffic signs
3. Ask for schedule and fare information

Unit 10 Optional Materials

● Picture cards and word cards for **train, subway, car, bus, bicycle, walk, drive,** and **ride.**

● Picture cards for Bus Stop, Walk, Don't Walk, Stop, One Way, Speed Limit, and No Parking signs. (You may be able to obtain good examples of the signs from your state's driver's manual.)

● Realia: Transportation tokens used in your community (if any) and/or coins to illustrate **fare;** bus maps and schedules.

♦ Blackline Master 10: Bus Map and Schedule, page 152.

COMPETENCIES (page 121)

Identify kinds of transportation

PRESENTATION

Teaching Note: Use this page to warm up students, to check and draw on their prior knowledge, and to spark interest.

Read the unit title and questions aloud. Encourage students to identify as many items in the picture as they can and to describe what is happening. As students may be able to say very little, you might have to prompt them by indicating items for them to name or by saying names of items and having students indicate them. Repeat students' ideas or restate them in acceptable English.

FOLLOW-UP

Transportation in Your Town: With students' help, make a simple sketch on the board or overhead projector of a busy intersection in your town. Use the illustration on this page as a guide. Encourage volunteers to identify the different kinds of transportation. Indicate each type of transportation in turn and ask students to raise their hands if they have used it.

♦ Ask, *What's the best way to go to (the store) in our town?* Write students' answers on the board or overhead projector. Then ask, *What were the best ways to go to (the store) in your country?* Encourage students to share their experiences.

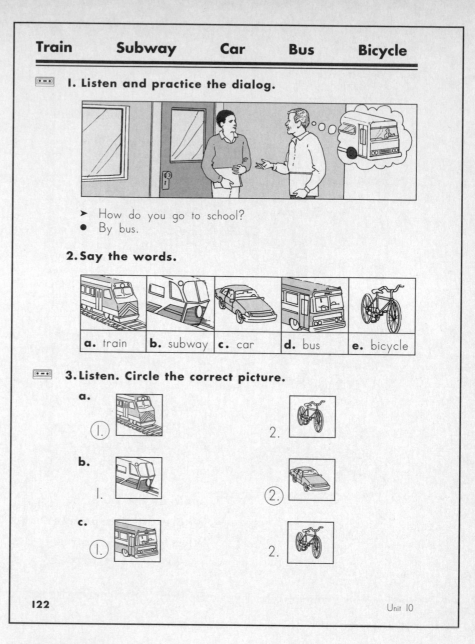

Train   Subway   Car   Bus   Bicycle

1. Listen and practice the dialog.

➤ How do you go to school?
● By bus.

2. Say the words.

| **a.** train | **b.** subway | **c.** car | **d.** bus | **e.** bicycle |

3. Listen. Circle the correct picture.

a. (1.) 2.

b. 1. (2.)

c. (1.) 2.

122   Unit 10

PREPARATION

Preteach the new language in the lesson. Follow these suggestions.

● Use picture cards and word cards and/or the illustrations in the book to preteach the recognition words **train, subway, car, bus,** and **bicycle.** See "Presenting Recognition Words" on page vii.

● Preteach the dialog. Draw a simple sketch of your school on the board. Hold up the picture card for the method of transportation you use to come to school, point to the sketch, and say, *I go to school by (method of transportation).* Then ask a volunteer, *How do you go to school?* Help the volunteer answer. Repeat with other volunteers.

PRESENTATION

1. Focus attention on the illustration. Have the students say as much as they can about it. You may want to cue them by indicating items for them to name or by saying names of items and having students indicate them. Restate students' ideas in acceptable English and write them on the board or overhead projector. Present the dialog. See "Presenting Dialogs" on page vii.

2. Help students read the directions. Discuss the pictures. Demonstrate by saying the names of the types of transportation with a volunteer. Then have students complete the exercise. Ask volunteers to say the words aloud to the class.

3. Help students read the directions.

Then present the listening. See "Presenting Listenings" on page vii. Ask volunteers to read the numbers of the correct answers aloud.

4. Help students read the directions. Demonstrate by completing the first item on the board or overhead projector. Then have students complete the exercise. Ask volunteers to circle answers on the board or overhead projector. Check students' work.

5. Help students read the directions. Demonstrate by completing the first item on the board or overhead projector. Then have students complete the exercise. Ask volunteers to write the answers on the board or overhead projector. Check students' work.

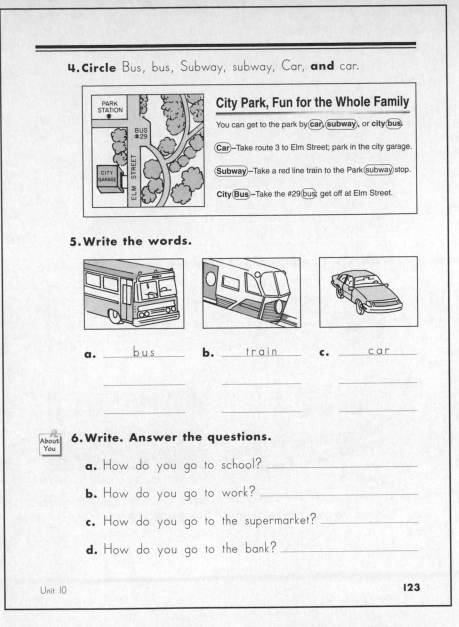

4. Circle Bus, bus, Subway, subway, Car, **and** car.

City Park, Fun for the Whole Family

You can get to the park by (car), (subway), or **city** (bus).

(Car)—Take route 3 to Elm Street; park in the city garage.

(Subway)—Take a red line train to the Park (subway) stop.

City (Bus)—Take the #29 (bus); get off at Elm Street.

5. Write the words.

a. _____ b u s _____ b. _____ t r a i n _____ c. _____ c a r _____

6. Write. Answer the questions.

a. How do you go to school? _____

b. How do you go to work? _____

c. How do you go to the supermarket? _____

d. How do you go to the bank? _____

Unit 10   **123**

---

6. Help students read the directions. Brainstorm with students all the possible choices for the answers and write them on the board or overhead projector. Demonstrate by answering the items with personal or fictitious information on the board or overhead projector. Then have students complete the exercise. Ask volunteers to read their answers aloud. Check students' work.

FOLLOW-UP

How Do You Go Places? On the board or overhead projector draw a chart on which to write the results of a survey of your class's methods of transportation. Label the vertical columns **bus, car, subway, train,** and **bicycle.** Label the horizontal rows **school, work, supermarket,** and **bank.** Ask students who take the bus to school to raise their hands. Tally the number, and write it in the appropriate box on the chart. Repeat for each combination of type of transportation and place.

♦ Provide students with paper and have them write these words in a list: **bus, car, subway, train, bicycle.** Then have students circulate to find a classmate who usually uses each type of transportation. The classmate signs his or her name next to the type of transportation.

Walk   Drive   Ride

I. Listen and practice the dialog.

➤ How do you go to school?
● I walk. How about you?
➤ I drive.

2. Work with a partner. Say the sentences.

a. She drives.   **b.** He walks.   **c.** He takes the bus.

d. She takes the train.   **e.** He rides his bicycle.

3. How do you go to school? Complete the sentence.

I _____ to school.

124   Unit 10

PREPARATION

Preteach the new language in the lesson. Follow these suggestions.

● Use word cards, picture cards, pantomime, and/or the illustrations in the book to preteach the recognition words **walk, drive,** and **ride.** See "Presenting Recognition Words" on page vii.

● Preteach the dialog. Review the phrase **How about you?** See "Presentation" on page 52.

PRESENTATION

1. Focus attention on the illustration. Have students say as much as they can about it. You may want to cue them by indicating items for them to name or by saying names of items and having students indicate them. Restate students' ideas in acceptable English and write them on the board or overhead projector.

Present the dialog. See "Presenting Dialogs" on page vii.

2. Have students read the directions. Model the first item with a partner. Then have the students complete the exercise in pairs. Ask volunteers to say the sentences to the class.

3. Help students read the directions. Demonstrate by completing the item on the board or overhead projector with personal or fictitious information. Then have students complete the exercise. Ask each student in turn to say his or her sentence to the class.

4. Help students read the directions. Demonstrate by writing your sentence on the board or overhead projector. Then have students complete the exercise independently. Check students' work.

5. Help students read the directions. Complete the first item on the board or overhead projector. Ask volunteers to read their answers aloud. Check students' work.

6. Help students read the directions, the question, and the categories. Complete the first item on the board or overhead projector using your own or a volunteer's information. Then have students complete the exercise. One at a time, name each person in the class and

About You 4. Write the sentence in 3.

_____

_____

About You 5. Write. Answer the questions.

   a. How do you go to school? _____

   b. How do you go to the supermarket? _____

   c. How do you go to the bank? _____

   d. How do you go to work? _____

About You 6. Work with a group. How do you go to school?
   Complete the chart.

NAME	CAR	BUS	WALK	SUBWAY	TRAIN	BICYCLE
Marion		✔				

Unit 10   **125**

ask the student who has his or her information to read it aloud. Check students' work.

FOLLOW-UP

Types of Transportation: Write the names of the types of transportation taught in this unit on separate index cards. Pantomime one of them and encourage students to figure out which type it is. When they answer correctly show them the card. Then give a card to each of several volunteers. Have individuals take turns pantomiming a type of transportation for the rest of the class to figure out.

♦ Have students brainstorm as many types of transportation as they can think of. Model words students want to know. Write the list on the board or overhead projector. Provide index cards and have each student write the name of one type of transportation. Then have students in small groups take turns pantomiming the types of transportation as the rest of the group tries to figure out which type it is.

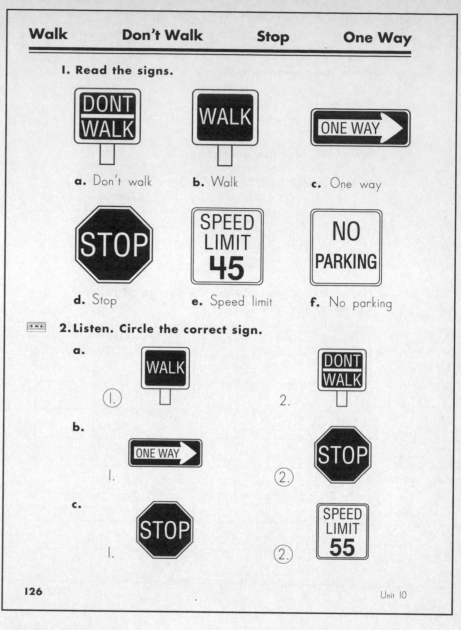

Walk   Don't Walk   Stop   One Way

1. Read the signs.

a. Don't walk   b. Walk   c. One way

d. Stop   e. Speed limit   f. No parking

2. Listen. Circle the correct sign.

a.
1. WALK   2. DONT WALK

b.
1. ONE WAY   2. STOP

c.
1. STOP   2. SPEED LIMIT 55

126   Unit 10

PREPARATION

Preteach the new language in the lesson. Follow these suggestions.

● Use word cards, picture cards, pantomime, and/or the illustrations in the book to preteach the recognition words **Walk, Don't Walk, Stop,** and **One Way.** See "Presenting Recognition Words" on page vii.

● Draw a simple street map on the board or overhead projector that includes the signs **Speed Limit 25** and **No Parking.** Move a picture of a car along the street and demonstrate how the car slows down to obey the speed limit and how the car avoids parking in the no-parking zone.

PRESENTATION

1. Focus attention on the signs. Help students read the labels aloud. Say the labels and have students identify the appropriate signs by letter. Then say the letters and have students name the signs.

2. Help students read the directions. Then present the listening. See "Presenting Listenings" on page vii. Ask volunteers to say the numbers of the correct answers aloud.

3. Help students read the directions. Demonstrate by completing the first item on the board or overhead projector. Have students complete the exercise. Check students' work.

4. Help students read the directions. Demonstrate by completing the first

item on the board or overhead projector. Have students complete the exercise in pairs. Ask volunteers to indicate the correct answers on the board or overhead projector. Check students' work.

5. Help students read the directions. Demonstrate by completing the first item on the board or overhead projector. Have students complete the exercise independently. Check students' work.

FOLLOW-UP

Around the Neighborhood: Take your students for a walk on the streets near your school. Have them look for street signs and read them. Ask questions such as, **What is the speed limit on this street? Can you**

3. Circle STOP, WALK, ONE WAY, **and** SPEED LIMIT.

4. Look at the pictures. Circle the words.

(ONE WAY)   (SPEED LIMIT 30)   (WALK)
WALK   ONE WAY   SPEED LIMIT 30

5. Write the words.

a. _walk_   **b.** _don't walk_   **c.** _speed limit_

park here? Can you cross the street
here?

♦ When you return to the classroom,
have students help you make a simple map of the streets around your
school on the board or overhead projector. Include street signs and traffic
lights.

Identify kinds of transportation

Read traffic signs

Ask for schedule and fare
information

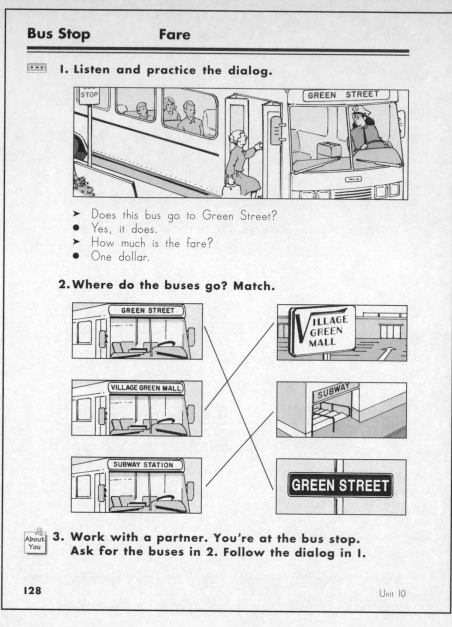

Bus Stop   Fare

▭ **I. Listen and practice the dialog.**

➤ Does this bus go to Green Street?
● Yes, it does.
➤ How much is the fare?
● One dollar.

2. Where do the buses go? Match.

GREEN STREET		VILLAGE GREEN MALL
VILLAGE GREEN MALL		SUBWAY
SUBWAY STATION		GREEN STREET

**3. Work with a partner. You're at the bus stop.
Ask for the buses in 2. Follow the dialog in I.**

128   Unit 10

PREPARATION

Preteach the new language in the
lesson. Follow these suggestions.

● Use picture cards and word cards
to preteach the recognition words
bus stop. Use a word card and play
or real coins and tokens to preteach
fare. See "Presenting Recognition
Words" on page vii.

● Preteach the dialog. On the board
or overhead projector, sketch a
street and label it **Green Street.** Then
hold up a picture of a bus and say,
Does this bus go to Green Street?
Have students repeat. Model the
answer, *(Yes, it does.)* Then "drive"
the picture of the bus to your sketch
of Green Street.

PRESENTATION

1. Focus attention on the illustration.
Have students say as much as they
can about it. You may want to cue
students by indicating items for them
to name or by saying names of items
and having students indicate them.
Restate students' ideas in acceptable
English and write them on the board
or overhead projector.

Present the dialog. See "Presenting
Dialogs" on page vii.

2. Help students read the directions.
Demonstrate by completing the first
item on the board or overhead projector. Then have the students complete the exercise in pairs. Check students' work.

3. Help students read the
directions. Demonstrate the
exercise with a volunteer. Take turns
beginning the dialog. Then have students complete the exercise in pairs.
Have them change partners and
repeat the exercise. Ask volunteers
to say their conversations for the
class.

4. Help students read the directions.
Demonstrate by completing the first
item on the board or overhead projector. Have students complete the
exercise independently. Check students' work.

5. Help students read the directions
for the first part of the exercise.
Then present the listening. See
"Presenting Listenings" on page
vii. Ask volunteers to read the cor-

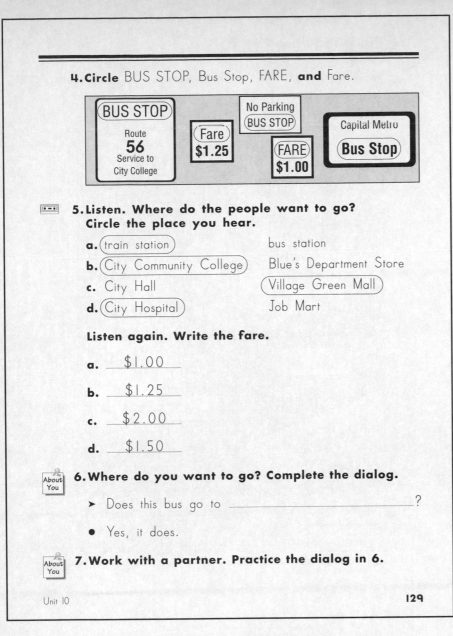

4. Circle BUS STOP, Bus Stop, FARE, **and** Fare.

BUS STOP
Route
56
Service to
City College

No Parking
BUS STOP

Fare
$1.25

FARE
$1.00

Capital Metro
Bus Stop

**5. Listen. Where do the people want to go?
Circle the place you hear.**

a. (train station)   bus station

b. (City Community College)   Blue's Department Store

c. City Hall   (Village Green Mall)

d. (City Hospital)   Job Mart

Listen again. Write the fare.

a. $1.00

b. $1.25

c. $2.00

d. $1.50

6. Where do you want to go? Complete the dialog.

➤ Does this bus go to _____?

● Yes, it does.

7. Work with a partner. Practice the dialog in 6.

Unit 10   129

---

rect answers aloud. Then read the directions for the second part of the exercise and repeat the procedure for presenting the listening.

6. Help students read the directions. Brainstorm with students possible bus destinations for places they might want to go in your area. Then demonstrate on the board or overhead projector by completing the sentence with a destination of your choice. Have students complete the exercise. Check students' work.

7. Help students read the directions. Demonstrate with a volunteer. Take turns beginning the dialog. Then have students complete the exercise. Ask volunteers to repeat their conversations for the class.

FOLLOW-UP

Bus Routes and Schedules:
Distribute copies of Blackline Master 10: Bus Map and Schedule. Help students look over the map. Have students identify the places and read the street names. Ask students to say whether they can ride the bus at certain times or to certain places. Ask, *It's (12:30) on (Sunday). Can you ride the bus? Can you ride the bus to the (airport)?*

♦ Distribute copies of a bus map and schedule for a bus that comes near your school. With students' help, find the stop closest to your school. Ask students when the bus stops near your school.

◆ Put It Together

Work with a partner. Write the words on the picture.

bicycle   bus   car   subway   train

4. subway

DOWNTOWN

GREEN STREET

2. bus

1. bicycle

3. car

5. train

PREPARATION

On the board or overhead projector, write the words **bicycle, bus, car, subway, train.** Ask volunteers to read the words aloud and find a picture card or illustration in their books to match each item.

PRESENTATION

Help students read the directions. Demonstrate by completing the first item on the board or overhead projector. Then have students complete the exercise in pairs. Ask volunteers to write their answers on the board or overhead projector.

FOLLOW-UP

Types of Transportation: Provide pairs of students with magazines that contain pictures of street scenes. Have them work in pairs to find pages with pictures of the types of transportation they learned in this unit. Ask pairs to show their pictures to the class and name the types of transportation.

◆ Brainstorm with students all the types of transportation in your town. Write the list on the board or overhead projector. Then ask students who have used each type to share their experiences with the class. If you can obtain telephone numbers for information about the types of transportation, write them on the board or overhead projector. Give students time to copy the telephone numbers they need.

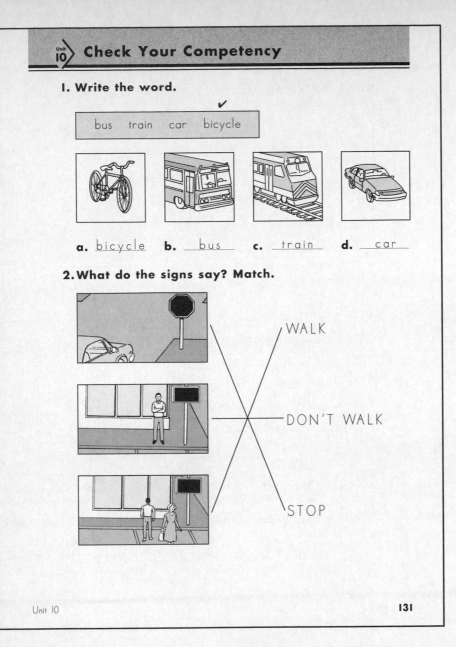

1. Write the word.

| bus   train   car   bicycle |

a. bicycle b. bus c. train d. car

2. What do the signs say? Match.

WALK

DON'T WALK

STOP

Unit 10   131

PREPARATION

Briefly review the new language in this unit before students open their books. Write the words on the board or overhead projector and ask volunteers to find the matching picture cards or to indicate appropriate illustrations in their books.

Review traffic signs and their meanings.

Provide specific help as needed until you are sure students feel confident that they know all the new words and signs.

PRESENTATION

Use any of the procedures in "Evaluation," page viii, with these pages. Record individuals' results on the Unit 10 Individual Competency Chart. Record the class's results on the Class Cumulative Competency Chart.

ENGLISH IN ACTION

An Optional Cooperative Learning Activity: Set up bus station "information booths" at several places around the room. Ask for a volunteer to staff each booth. Provide these volunteers with copies of your local area's bus route and schedule or with copies of Blackline Master 10. Ask the rest of the students to visit one of the booths and ask questions about where the bus stops and/or what time it stops at a specific location. Demonstrate by asking a few questions yourself. As an exten-sion of this activity, you might wish to accompany your students on a visit to a nearby bus or train station.

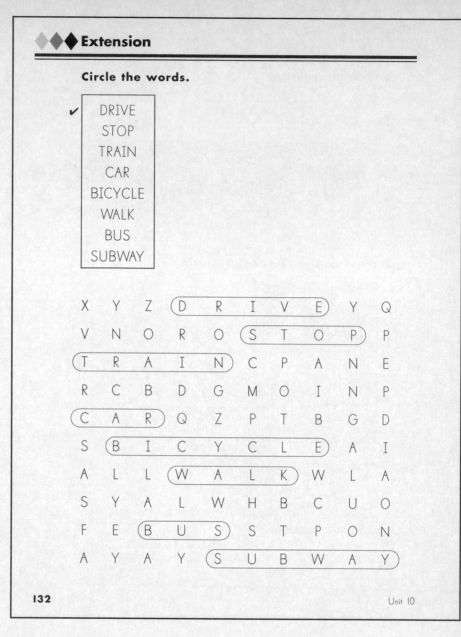

Circle the words.

✔
DRIVE
STOP
TRAIN
CAR
BICYCLE
WALK
BUS
SUBWAY

X Y Z (D R I V E) Y Q
V N O R O (S T O P) P
(T R A I N) C P A N E
R C B D G M O I N P
(C A R) Q Z P T B G D
S (B I C Y C L E) A I
A L L (W A L K) W L A
S Y A L W H B C U O
F E (B U S) S T P O N
A Y A Y (S U B W A Y)

132   Unit 10

PREPARATION

Write **DIDRIVEDE** on the board in letters approximately the same size as those on the word card for **DRIVE.** Hold the word card against the first five letters on the board, shake your head, and say *No.* Move the card so it lines up with **IDRIV** and repeat your rejection of the match. Move the card again so that it lines up with **DRIVE.** This time indicate your acceptance of the match.

PRESENTATION

Help students read the directions. Demonstrate by circling **DRIVE** on the board.

Have students complete the word puzzle activity in pairs. Circulate to assist as needed.

Copy the puzzle on the board or overhead projector. Have volunteers come forward, one at a time, to circle the correct answer for each item. Check students' work.

Listening Transcript

Page 12

Exercise 3. Listen for *name*. Raise your hand.

a. A: What's your name?
   B: George Smith.
b. A: Who's that man?
   B: George Smith.
c. A: Who is she?
   B: Ellen Porch.
d. A: What do I do next?
   B: Please write your name on the line.
e. A: Hi. I'm Joe.
   B: Hi. I'm Barbara.

Page 14

Exercise 3. Listen. Circle the word you hear.

a. A: What's your last name?
   B: My last name is Soto.
b. A: Do you know her name?
   B: Yes. Her name is Mary.
c. A: Write your last name on the form.
   B: Excuse me?
   A: Write your last name.

Page 16

Exercise 3. Listen. Circle the word you hear.

a. A: What's her address?
   B: Her address is 38 Rockwood Road.
   A: Do you know what city that's in?
b. A: He lives on Green Road.
   B: Do you know what number on Green Road?
   A: Number 10.
c. A: What street does Tim live on?
   B: I think he lives on Brown Street.

Page 18

Exercise 3. Listen for *zip code*. Raise your hand.

a. A: What's your zip code?
   B: 33056.
b. A: What's your name?
   B: My name is Tanya.
c. A: My zip code is 87730.
   B: What city is that?
   A: Santa Fe.
d. A: What's your address?
   B: 45 Main Street.

Page 20

Exercise 3. Listen for *telephone number*. Raise your hand.

a. A: What's his address?
   B: 35 Riverside Drive.
b. A: What's your telephone number?
   B: 555-1238.
c. A: What's your last name?
   B: Dalton.
d. A: My telephone number is 503-555-0112.
   B: OK. Thanks.

Page 28

Exercise 3. Listen. Circle the place you hear.

a. A: Where's the police station?
   B: The police station? It's on Green Street.
b. A: I want to mail a letter. Where's the post office?
   B: The post office is on Green Street, I think.
c. A: I think the bank is on Brown Street.
   B: No. The bank's on Green Street.

Page 31

Exercise 5. Listen. Circle the word you hear.

a. A: Excuse me. Could you tell me where the post office is?
   B: Sure. The post office is two blocks down on the right.
   A: Thanks.
b. A: Oh, no. I'm out of stamps.
   B: I have some. How many stamps do you need?
   A: Only two.
   B: Here you go.

A: Thanks.

c. A: We have to mail the letter to George. Where's a mailbox?

B: There's a mailbox on Green Street.

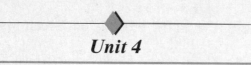

Unit 3

Page 42

Exercise 3. Listen. Circle the word you hear.

a. A: Do you know where the men's room is?

B: Yes. The men's room is on the left, next to room 23.

b. A: Where's the women's room?

B: The women's room is down the hall on the right, next to room 20.

A: Thanks.

c. A: I'm looking for the office.

B: The office is in room 22, on the right.

A: Thanks.

Page 45

Exercise 5. Listen. Circle the number.

a. John, please sit at this desk.

b. Please open your books.

Unit 4

Page 50

Exercise 3. Listen. Circle the times you hear.

a. A: Oh, I'm going to be late for work. What time is it?

B: Don't worry. It's only 7:30.

A: Only 7:30? It's early.

b. A: Excuse me. When does the next train arrive?

B: It should be here at 9:00.

A: 9:00? Thanks.

c. A: There's a movie for the kids at the library tomorrow. Do you want to come?

B: What time?

A: 3:30.

B: That sounds like fun. I'll meet you there at 3:30.

d. A: Wake up! It's 7:00. It's time to get ready for school.

B: I'm tired. Do I have to?

A: Yes. It's 7:00. You have to get up.

Page 53

Exercise 5. Listen. Circle the days you hear.

a. A: Are we in the same English class?

B: I don't know. When's your class?

A: On Tuesday night. How about you?

B: My class is on Tuesday, too. I guess we're in the same class.

b. A: What day do you have off this week?

B: Thursday.

A: Really? Do you want to go to the movies on Thursday?

B: Sure. That'd be great.

c. A: Do you want to go out for lunch on Sunday?

B: I'm sorry, I can't. I usually visit my mother on Sunday.

d. A: My son's playing baseball on Saturday. Can you come to the game?

B: What time does the game start? I work on Saturday morning.

A: 2:00.

B: Great. I'll be there.

Page 54

Exercise 3. Listen. Circle the date you hear.

a. A: Hi, Sally. I want to invite you to a party we're having.

B: Great. When is it?

A: July third.

B: Oh, that's too bad. We'll be away on July third. I'm afraid that we can't come.

A: Sorry you'll have to miss it.

B: Me, too.

b. A: I'm calling to make an appointment with Dr. Martin.

B: When would you like to see her?

A: The second week in June.
B: How's June ninth at 2:00?
A: June ninth is fine. Thanks.
c. A: I sure could use a day off from work.
B: Me, too. We haven't had a day off for a couple of months.
A: Well, Columbus Day is only a few days away.
B: When's that?
A: October twelfth.
B: That's soon enough. October twelfth is next week.
d. A: When can I see the dentist?
B: How about July fifteenth?
A: No. July fifteenth is my birthday. I don't want to go to the dentist on my birthday.

Unit 5

Page 63
Exercise 3. Listen. Circle the number of the food you hear.

a. A: I have to stop at the supermarket.
B: What do you need?
A: A dozen eggs.
b. A: What do you want for dinner tonight?
B: How about chicken? I think I have a chicken in the freezer.
A: That sounds great.
c. A: What's left on the list?
B: A carton of milk.
A: Milk? I'll get it. The dairy section is over there. I'll meet you at the front of the store.

Page 65
Exercise 6. Listen. Circle the aisle number you hear.

a. A: Excuse me. Where's the detergent?
B: Aisle 2.
A: Aisle 2? Thanks.
b. A: We have to get bread and oranges.
B: The fruit and vegetables section is on aisle 3.

A: Where?
B: Aisle 3.
c. A: Let's see. I have to get rice and cereal. Do you know where the cereal is?
B: I'm not sure. Oh look, there's a sign. It says cereal's on aisle 6.
A: Aisle 6. Thanks.

Unit 6

Page 75
Exercise 5. Listen. Circle the number.

a. A: How much are the socks?
B: $2.95.
A: I'll take them.
B: Cash or charge?
A: Cash, please.
b. A: This coat is nice. How much is it?
B: $38.00.
A: Do you take charge cards?
B: Yes, we do.
c. A: The total for your shoes is $21.75. How would you like to pay?
B: Can I write a check?
A: Yes, but I'll need to see some ID.
B: That's fine. I have my license right here.

Page 77
Exercise 5. Listen. Circle the amount you hear.

a. A: How much is the paint?
B: $21.99.
b. A: Will that be cash or check?
B: What was the total?
A: $15.00.
B: I think I'll write a check.
c. A: I'm just going to stop and buy a hammer. They're on sale.
B: Really? How much? I need a hammer, too.
A: $8.50.
B: That's not much of a sale.

Unit 7

Page 86
Exercise 3. Listen. Circle the answer.

a. A: Where do you live, Manuel?
   B: I have an apartment on Green Street.
b. A: I went to Sandra's house yesterday.
   B: Where does she live?
   A: She lives over on Main Street.
   B: What's her house like?
   A: Oh, it's beautiful.
c. A: Hi, Mike. Would you like to go with us to the movies this afternoon?
   B: Yeah. That sounds like fun.
   A: OK. We can pick you up if you like. Where do you live?
   B: 12 Oak Street, apartment 33.
   A: Fine. We'll be there in about an hour.

Page 88
Exercise 3. Listen. Circle the room you hear.

a. A: I'm so tired I can hardly keep my eyes open.
   B: Why don't you go into the bedroom and take a nap?
   A: That's a good idea. I think I will.
b. A: Where's Dad?
   B: I'm not sure. Did you look in the kitchen? Maybe he's cooking dinner.
c. A: We need to clean the house before our party.
   B: I'll clean the bathroom.
   A: OK. I'll vacuum.

Page 90
Exercise 3. Listen. Circle the item you hear.

a. A: May I help you?
   B: Yes. I need a new stove. Do you have any stoves on sale?
   A: Yes. We have several models on sale this week.
b. A: How do you like your new house?

B: It's great. I just need a few pieces of furniture.
A: What do you need?
B: Well, to begin with, a new chair for the living room.
c. A: Bell's Appliance Repair. May I help you?
   B: Yes. My refrigerator isn't working. Can someone come by and take a look at it?
   A: Certainly. What's the address?
   B: 12 Oak Street, apartment 33.
   A: We'll send someone over this afternoon.
   B: Thanks.

Page 93
Exercise 5. Listen. Circle *rent* or *deposit*.

a. A: We found a great apartment.
   B: Where?
   A: On Brown Street.
   B: How many bedrooms?
   A: Two bedrooms and one bathroom.
   B: How's the rent?
   A: Pretty good. $425 a month.
b. A: Do you like the apartment?
   B: Yes, but I'm not sure I can afford it. Is there a deposit?
   A: Yes. $175.
   B: $175?
   A: Yes.
c. A: It's not easy to find an apartment for six people.
   B: I know. We were lucky to find one with three bedrooms.
   A: How much is the rent?
   B: $650.
   A: $650? Wow, that's high.

Unit 8

Page 99
Exercise 6. Listen. Circle the word you hear.

a. A: What happened?
   B: He slipped on the wet floor.
   A: Is he OK?

B: No. He hurt his arm. I think we should take him to the emergency room.

b. A: Help!

B: What happened?

A: I cut my hand on the broken glass!

B: Oh, my! That looks pretty bad. We'd better go to the hospital.

c. A: Mom, I cut my foot.

B: Let me see.

A: It hurts.

B: It's not a bad cut. Let me wash it and put a bandage on it.

Page 101
Exercise 6. Listen. When will the people see the doctor? Circle the answers.

a. A: Dr. Franklin's office. May I help you?

B: Yes. I need to make an appointment to have my eyes checked.

A: Can you come in on Tuesday?

B: What time?

A: 10:30.

B: OK. Tuesday at 10:30.

b. A: Can I make an appointment to see the dentist?

B: Sure. How about Wednesday at 10:00?

A: That'll be fine.

B: OK. We'll see you Wednesday, April 16 at 10:00 A.M.

c. A: Do you think you can give me a ride to the clinic?

B: Sure. When do you need to go?

A: I have an appointment Monday at 4:45.

Page 103
Exercise 6. Listen. What's the matter? Circle the answers.

a. A: I think we should take the baby to the doctor.

B: Why?

A: She has a sore throat.

B: Maybe she has a cold.

A: Let's call the doctor and ask.

b. A: I feel awful.

B: What's the matter?

A: I have a terrible headache.

B: Why don't you take some aspirin?

c. A: I have to call the doctor.

B: What's the matter? Are you sick?

A: Yes. I have a really bad stomachache.

Page 104
Exercise 3. Listen. How much medicine do they take? Check the box.

a. A: Jung, you don't look well. Are you sick?

B: Yes. I went to see the doctor this morning.

A: Did she give you any medicine?

B: Yes. She gave me a prescription. I have to take two capsules three times a day.

b. A: I just got a prescription for my cough.

B: How much do you need to take?

A: It says two teaspoons every four hours.

c. A: Here's your prescription, Iris.

B: Thanks. How much do I take?

A: Take two tablets every six hours.

B: OK. Thanks.

d. A: Ms. Parker, here's Pat's prescription.

B: How much does Pat take?

A: Give him two tablespoons every morning before breakfast.

Unit 9

Page 110
Exercise 3. Listen. Circle the job you hear.

a. A: Oh, I'm tired.

B: Why?

A: I have a new job as a cook, and I'm on my feet all day.

B: Well, do you like the work?

A: Yes. Even though it's hard, I enjoy it.

b. A: Have you found a job yet?

B: Yes. I finally got a job at the Shaw Company.

A: Doing what?
B: I'm a file clerk.
A: That sounds great. Congratulations.
c. A: How's your brother?
B: He's fine. He just got a good job.
A: Really? What's he doing?
B: He's an auto mechanic at Silvio's Garage.

Page 112
Exercise 4. Listen. Do they have any work experience? Circle *Yes* or *No.*

a. A: I'm calling about the ad for a gardener.
B: Do you have any experience?
A: Yes. Before I came to this country, I was a gardener for many years.
B: Great. Can you come in later today for an interview?
A: Sure.
b. A: Hope Hospital. May I help you?
B: Yes. I saw your ad for a housekeeper. I'd like to apply for the job. Can you tell me about it?
A: Well, it's a part-time position, and the salary is $5.50 an hour. Do you have any experience?
B: No, I don't. Is that a problem?
A: No, it's OK. Experience isn't required. We have a training program for people without experience.
B: That sounds great.
c. A: Look at this ad, May. It's a perfect job for you.
B: What kind of job is it?
A: The American Cafe is looking for a full-time cook with experience working in a restaurant.
B: That sounds perfect. I worked at the Pickwick Restaurant for three years. Is there a phone number I can call?

Page 122
Exercise 3. Listen. Circle the correct picture.

a. A: Hurry up! The train's coming.
B: We'd better run.
b. A: I have to go downtown tomorrow. Can you give me a ride?
B: I'm sorry, I can't. My car's in the shop getting fixed.
c. A: How are you going to the game?
B: We're going to take the bus.

Page 126
Exercise 2. Listen. Circle the correct sign.

a. A: Be careful when you cross the street.
B: Don't worry. I'll be careful.
A: Only cross when the sign says WALK.
b. A: I saw a terrible accident.
B: What happened?
A: A car went through a stop sign and hit another car.
c. A: You'd better slow down. You're going too fast.
B: No, I'm not. The speed limit's 55.

Page 129
Exercise 5. Listen. Where do the people want to go? Circle the place you hear.

a. A: Excuse me. Does this bus go to the train station?
B: Yes. It leaves for the station every 15 minutes.
A: And could you tell me the fare?
B: That'll be $1.00.
b. A: Which bus do I take to get to City Community College?

B: The blue bus just up ahead will take you there, but you'll have to hurry. It's about to leave.

A: I'd better run then. I hope I have enough money with me. Do you know how much the fare is?

B: $1.25.

A: Thanks.

c. A: Excuse me. Does this bus go to Village Green Mall?

B: Yes. The mall is our first stop.

A: I know the fare is $2.00. Do I need exact change?

B: Yes, you do.

d. A: I got a new job at City Hospital. Do you know what bus I take to get there?

B: The bus on the corner goes to City Hospital.

A: By any chance, do you know how much the fare is?

B: $1.50.

A: Thanks.

Listen again. Write the fare. *[Play the tape or read the transcript for Exercise 5 aloud again.]*

Blackline Masters ◆ To The Teacher

The blackline masters on pages 142–152 allow for additional review and enrichment. Because you can make as many copies as you need, you can use them for a variety of purposes throughout the book:

♦ Students who complete individual, pair, or small group activities before the rest of the class can complete a blackline master activity independently.

♦ In open-entry/open-exit programs, use the blackline masters to provide any needed review as new students join the class.

♦ Use the blackline masters as games or for pair work.

♦ Have students complete a blackline master activity as review before the Check Your Competency page.

♦ You can assign them as homework.

Here are a few specific suggestions on ways you can use each blackline master. Feel free to think of additional activities of your own.

Blackline Master 1: Identification Form

♦ To help students generalize that different forms ask for the same information, have students look at both forms. Say **name** and have them point to it on both forms. Continue with the other information on the forms.

♦ Have students fill out the forms independently.

♦ Have pairs interview each other and complete one of the forms for their partners.

Blackline Master 2: Telephone

♦ Have students practice dialing telephone numbers. Say telephone numbers aloud and have students touch the numbers on the keypad. Use the numbers of businesses, service agencies, long distance numbers, 800 numbers, 911, directory assistance, the school's

office or attendance office, their employers (for reporting absences), the poison control center, and so on. Individuals might say their telephone numbers for the others to dial.

♦ To reinforce letters of the alphabet, have students look at the telephone and find which letters are not on the keypad (**Q** and **Z**).

♦ To reinforce letters and/or numbers, use correction fluid to delete several letters and/or numbers on a photocopy of the master. Then duplicate a copy for every student. Have students fill in the missing information.

Blackline Master 3: Classroom Objects

♦ Have students cut out the pictures and use them to start personal picture dictionaries or to make flash cards. (For instructions, see page vii of the Introduction to the Literacy Level.)

♦ Have students label the pictures.

♦ Divide the class into teams. Give each team a copy of the blackline master. Have each team collect as many of the actual objects as they can. Have each team report how many of each object they have, "We have (three) erasers."

Blackline Master 4: Clock

♦ Give each student a copy of the blackline master. Help them cut out the hands and mount them with brads. Then say times and have students display the time on their clocks. Check to make sure everyone has the correct time.

Blackline Master 5: Money

♦ Use the money to teach students how to say amounts of money. Display various amounts and say how much money you have, such as three hundred dollars. Have students repeat.

♦ Set up a classroom store, supermarket, or mall. Students can use the money to pay for purchases.

Blackline Master 6: Blank Check

♦ Use an overhead transparency of the master to model how to write and endorse checks.

♦ Make multiple copies and have students use them to "pay" various bills, such as utility bills, rent payments, and so on. You might bring in, or have students bring in, real bills for them to look at and pay with the checks.

♦ Bring in mail order catalogs. Have the class imagine that they are going to buy an item. Help them make a selection, complete the order form, and pay with one of the checks.

Blackline Masters 7a and b: House and Furniture

♦ Give each student copies of the masters. Give instructions about how to place the furniture in the rooms. When everyone has finished, have pairs compare their arrangements to make sure that they are the same.

♦ Have students use the furniture pictures in their personal picture dictionaries. (See page vii of the Introduction to the Literacy Level.)

♦ Have students use the money from **Blackline Master 5** and the furniture and to set up a furniture store. Help students put prices on the furniture. Give each student a certain amount of money, such as $500, to furnish their homes. Have them go shopping in pairs or in small groups, make their purchases, and pay for them. Appoint clerks to help the customers. Have students arrange their purchases in their homes and describe them to the class.

Blackline Master 8: Human Body

♦ Have students use a copy of the blackline master in their personal picture dictionaries. (See page vii of the Introduction to the Literacy Level.)

♦ Use the blackline master to play a variety of Simon Says games. For example, give each student a copy of the unlabeled human body.

Say, "Simon says, 'Point to the head.'" Have students respond by pointing to the head. Any students who follow an instruction not prefaced by "Simon says" must stop playing.

You might also have students play using the labeled human body. Give instructions as before and have students point to the correct word except when the instruction is not prefaced by "Simon says."

♦ To reinforce listening and writing skills, give each student a copy of the unlabeled picture. Dictate the names of the body parts in random order and have students write them on the correct lines. Check students' work.

Blackline Master 9: Job Application

♦ Have students complete the application about themselves. Then collect the completed applications, check them, and return them to students with another copy of the application. Have them complete the second application with the corrected information. Check their work. Remind them to carry this application with them when applying for jobs to help them complete the applications quickly and accurately.

♦ Have pairs interview each other and complete the application for their partners.

Blackline Master 10: Bus Schedule

♦ Have students look over the map and schedule. Have them use it to plan trips to various places and at various times of day. Check to make sure that all of the trips are possible.

♦ Students might use the map and schedule as a model to create maps and schedules for a real or imaginary bus route in their city or town.

Each unit of the Teacher's Edition contains additional ideas for using the blackline masters.

IDENTIFICATION FORM

Name	
Address	
City	State
Zip Code	Telephone Number

IDENTIFICATION FORM

NAME

ADDRESS

CITY   STATE   ZIP CODE

TELEPHONE NUMBER

IMPORTANT TELEPHONE NUMBERS	
Police	**911**
Fire Department	**911**
Ambulance	**911**

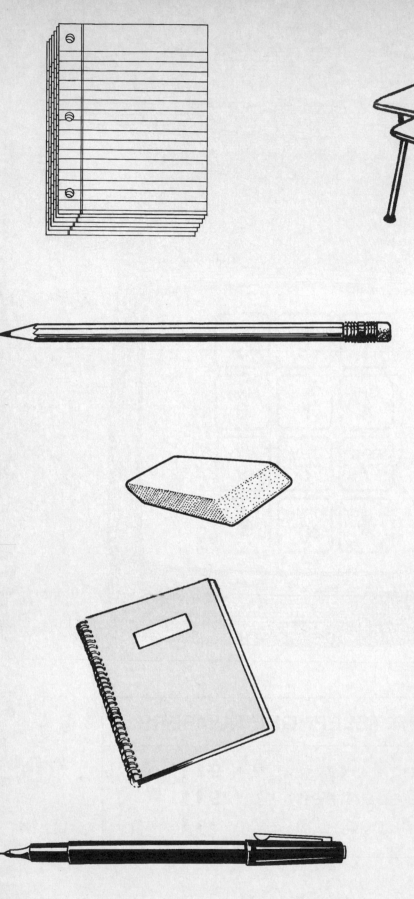

Blackline Master 3: Classroom Objects

Blackline Master 4: Clock

Blackline Master 5: Money

550

_____

_____ 19 _____

PAY TO THE
ORDER OF _____ $ [_____]

_____ DOLLARS

✳CITYBANK
CITYBANK of AMERICA

_____

MEMO

551

_____

_____ 19 _____

PAY TO THE
ORDER OF _____ $ [_____]

_____ DOLLARS

✳CITYBANK
CITYBANK of AMERICA

_____

MEMO

ENDORSE HERE

X ____

DO NOT WRITE BELOW THIS LINE

Blackline Master 6: Blank Check

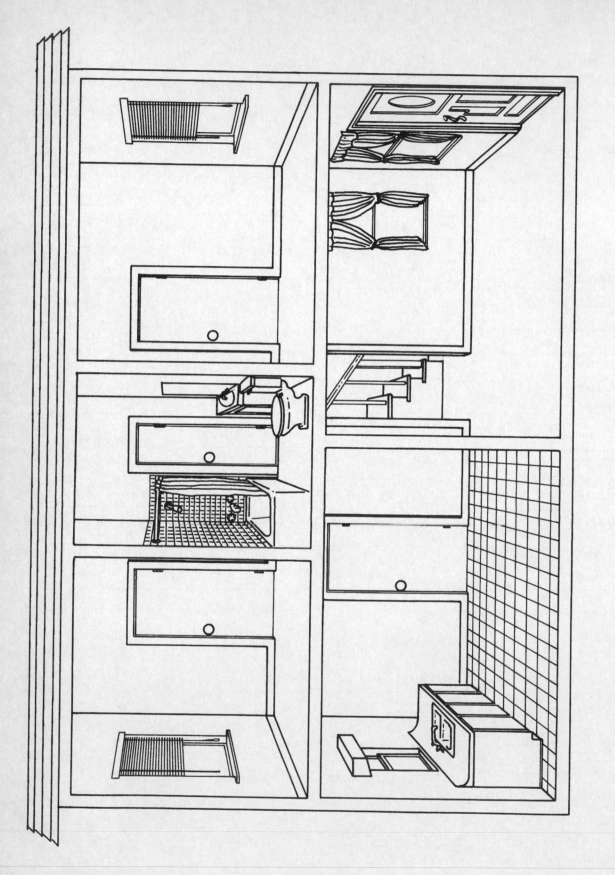

Blackline Master 7a: Rooms

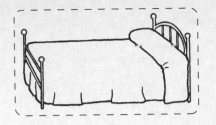

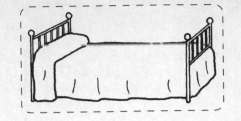

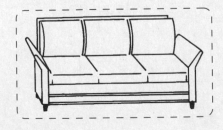

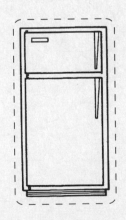

Blackline Master 7b: Furniture

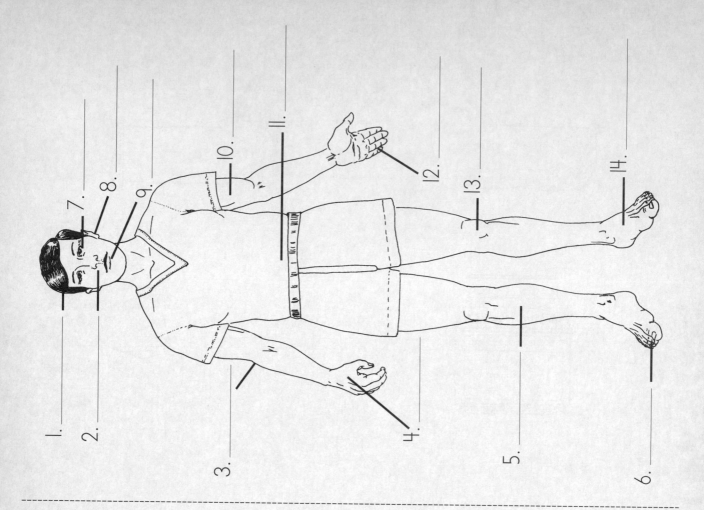

Head
Eye
Nose
Ear
Mouth

Arm
Stomach

Elbow

Hand

Finger

Knee

Leg

Foot

Toe

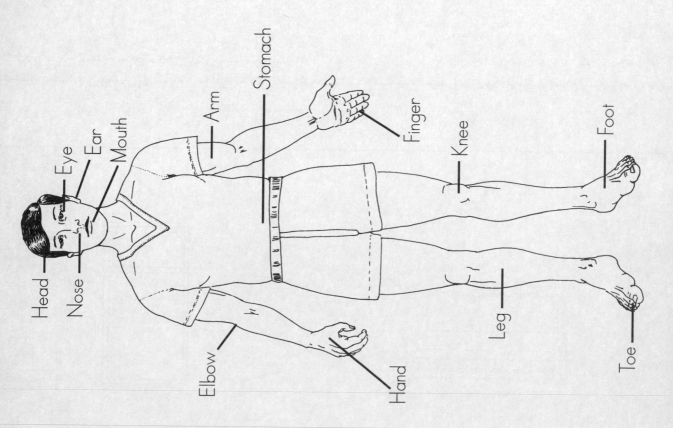

1.
2.
7.
8.
9.
10.
11.
3.
4.
12.
13.
5.
14.
6.

THE Star COMPANY

APPLICATION FOR EMPLOYMENT

Name:

Social Security Number:

Telephone Number:

Address:

Position applied for:

Date you can start:

Salary expected:

_____ an hour _____ a month _____ a year

☐ Full time

☐ Part time—If part time, hours you can work:

Monday—Friday: _____ Saturday/Sunday: _____

List any friends and/or relatives working with us now:

Are you over 21?   Yes ☐   No ☐

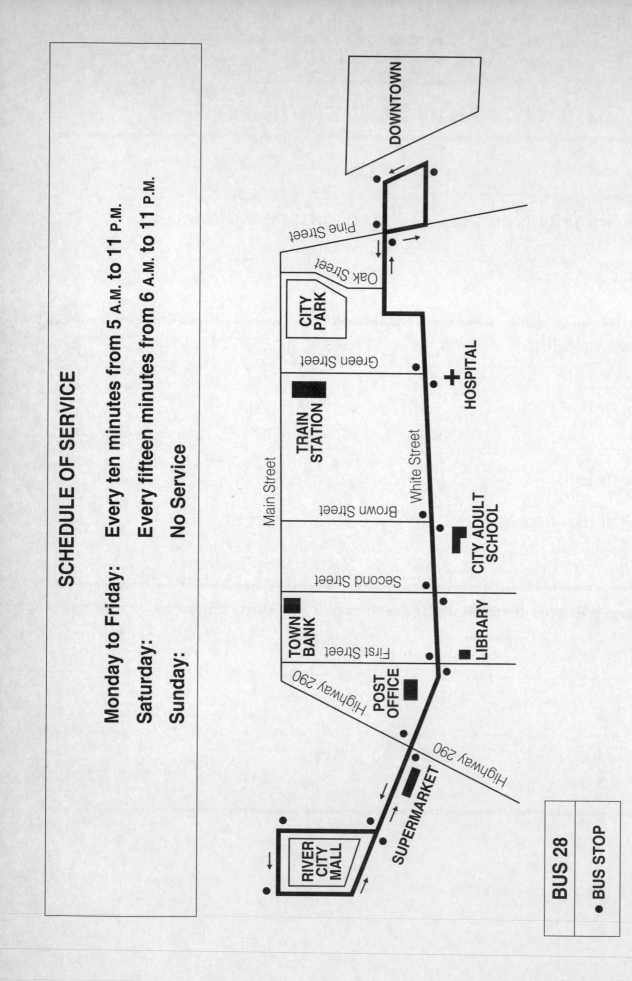

SCHEDULE OF SERVICE

Monday to Friday: Every ten minutes from 5 A.M. to 11 P.M.

Saturday: Every fifteen minutes from 6 A.M. to 11 P.M.

Sunday: No Service

DOWNTOWN

Pine Street

Oak Street

CITY PARK

Green Street

HOSPITAL

TRAIN STATION

Main Street

White Street

Brown Street

CITY ADULT SCHOOL

Second Street

TOWN BANK

LIBRARY

First Street

Highway 290

POST OFFICE

Highway 290

SUPERMARKET

RIVER CITY MALL

BUS 28

● BUS STOP

Individual Competency Chart

Student _____

Class _____

Teacher _____

Literacy Level ♦ Unit 1

Competencies	Date Checked	Result (✔)	Comments
Competencies			
Recognition Words			

Literacy Level ♦ Unit 2

Competencies	Date Checked	Result (✔)	Comments
Competencies			
Recognition Words			

Individual Competency Chart

Student _____

Class _____

Teacher _____

Literacy Level ♦ Unit 3

Competencies	Date Checked	Result (✔)	Comments
Recognition Words			

Literacy Level ♦ Unit 4

Competencies	Date Checked	Result (✔)	Comments
Recognition Words			

Individual Competency Chart

Student _____ _____

Class _____

Teacher _____

Literacy Level ♦ Unit 5

Competencies	Date Checked	Result (✔)	Comments
Recognition Words			

Literacy Level ♦ Unit 6

Competencies	Date Checked	Result (✔)	Comments
Recognition Words			

Individual Competency Chart

Student _____

Class _____

Teacher _____

Literacy Level ◆ Unit 7

Competencies	Date Checked	Result (✔)	Comments
Recognition Words			

Literacy Level ◆ Unit 8

Competencies	Date Checked	Result (✔)	Comments
Recognition Words			

Real-Life English

Individual Competency Chart

Student _____

Class _____

Teacher _____

Literacy Level ◆ Unit 9

Competencies	Date Checked	Result (✔)	Comments
Recognition Words			

Literacy Level ◆ Unit 10

Competencies	Date Checked	Result (✔)	Comments
Recognition Words			

Class Cumulative Competency Chart

Literacy Level ♦ Unit _____   Class _____

Teacher _____

Competencies

Name								Comments